SNOWMALLOWS

Snowmallows

* * *

Carol Ann Soisson

SHEPHERD'S COMPANION PRESS,
LLC / STRATFORD, CT

Carol Ann Soisson/Shepherd's Companion Press, LLC
7365 Main Street # 317
Stratford, CT 06614

www.shepherdscompanion.com

Publisher's Cataloging-in-Publication Data
Names: Soisson, Carol Ann, author.
Title: Snowmallows / Carol Ann Soisson.
Description: Stratford, CT: Shepherd's Companion Press, LLC, 2020.
Summary: Sixth-grader David Griffin uses the Snowmallows causing a huge snowstorm. David works to stop the storm and repair his relationship with his Grandfather.
Identifiers: LCCN: 2020900097 | ISBN: 978-1-7343716-0-4 (Hardcover) | 978-1-7343716-1-1 (pbk.) | 978-1-7343716-2-8 (epub) | 978-1-7343716-3-5 (Mobi) | 978-1-7343716-4-2 (Kindle)
Subjects: LCSH Grandparents--Juvenile fiction. | Weather--Juvenile fiction. | Blizzards--Juvenile fiction. | Meteorology--Juvenile fiction. | Meteorologists--Juvenile fiction. | Family--Juvenile fiction. | Friendship--Juvenile fiction. | Brothers and sisters--Juvenile fiction. | Baseball--Juvenile fiction. | Christian fiction. | CYAC Grandparents--Fiction. | Weather--Fiction. | Blizzards--Fiction. | Meteorology--Fiction. | Meteorologists--Fiction. | Family--Fiction. | Friendship--Fiction. | Brothers and sisters--Fiction. | Baseball--Fiction. | BISAC JUVENILE FICTION / Science & Nature / Weather | JUVENILE FICTION / Family / Multigenerational | JUVENILE FICTION / Religious / Christian / General
Classification: LCC PZ7.1.S6625 Sn 2020 | DDC [Fic]--dc23

Book design © 2017 BookDesignTemplates.com

Printed in the United States of America. First printing February 2020

Contents

For everyone who hoped and believed with me that this book was possible, especially Don

CHAPTER 1

Friday, March 1 – Mid-Afternoon

School, unfortunately, was in session. So, I, even more unfortunately, had to suffer through a sixth-grade science class on weather. What twelve-year-old in Connecticut wants to be stuck in class when there is a warm, sunny, early March afternoon just outside the window? And who wants to study a subject that even adults only talk about when they have nothing else to say to one another? (Well, most adults. My boring grandfather is a weather scientist, so he talks about it all the time.) I needed to escape from the weather study inside to the real weather outside, so I slipped into my favorite daydream...

Here we are at what could be the last pitch of this championship series. The Titans have swept the first three games and now it's the last inning of game four. The score is one to zero in favor of the Titans, there are no men on base, and the batter has two strikes. Griffin is still on the mound. The rookie pitcher has done an incredible job for the Titans since coming up from the minors just a few short months ago. If not for him and his famous fastball, they may not have made it into the series at all. And now, here we are in the bottom of the ninth and he's on the verge of pitching a perfect game.

Griffin takes his stance. He winds up and tosses the pitch. It's a "Griffin's Greatest" fastball right over home plate. The batter swings...and misses! The Titans take the championship and David Griffin becomes one of the few people ever in the history of baseball to pitch a perfect game in post-season play! The crowd is chanting 'MVP!'. Undoubtedly, David Griffin will be the MVP of this series...

"Earth to David Griffin..." Ms. Fredericks' voice startled me from my favorite daydream.

"Sorry, Ms. Fredericks. I got a little distracted."

I swiveled around in my chair when I realized I was facing toward the window. Now I saw the weather-related swirls and charts on the board. I frowned. It was so much nicer staring out the window.

Ms. Fredericks walked over to my desk while the rest of the class worked in pairs on some review questions. "Your mind out on the ball field again?"

My blonde head bobbed up and down like the plastic Titan player with the big head on the dashboard of my Dad's car. "My team won the world championship again, thanks to me."

"Grand slam in game seven?" asked Ms. Fredericks.

"You'd think, but no. Pitched a perfect game in the last game of a four-game sweep."

"Impressive. That's a tough feat to accomplish."

"I think it's every pitcher's dream," I sighed. "At least, I know it's mine."

"It's a wonderful dream, David. But, before it can happen, you need to pass Monday's science test. You know this test can make or break your grade for the marking period, right?"

A chill ran down my back. "The big science test is THIS Monday? You mean three days from now?"

Ms. Fredericks sighed softly. She began rubbing her temples the way my Mom does when she's getting a headache. "Yes. Now, please, try to focus."

For the next half hour, I stared at the weather terms Ms. Fredericks wrote in multiple colors of marker on the white board at the front of the room. The rainbow of terms didn't clear the cloud of confusion and worry in my head. There was no way I could learn all this stuff with only two days to study. I needed a miracle.

Ms. Fredericks looked up at the clock. She gently set her blue marker down on the tray at the bottom of the board. "I think you've all suffered long enough. So, the last class of the week will be recess. And since it's such a beautiful day, we're going to play a little baseball outside."

My ears heard something I understood for the first time in hours. My hand shot into the air. The thought of playing my favorite sport during my favorite class revived me. "Ms. Fredericks, can I pitch?" I was so excited, I asked without her calling on me.

"Not again," said Cassie.

"Nobody gets a hit when he pitches," said Evan. "We're not even close."

"I'm not catching. He threw one of those 'Griffin's Greatest Fastballs' one time when I was catcher, and it almost killed me," said Henry, who was also known as Drama because of his tendency to exaggerate everything. "I think I might still have scars."

Cassie lifted an eyebrow at him. "Really, Drama? Scars?"

"Mental scars," said Drama as he stared off into the distance.

Listening to them, I tried not to roll my eyes. What a bunch of babies, being afraid of my fastball. Then again, I probably shouldn't judge. I've never had to catch a "Griffin's Greatest".

Ms. Fredericks held up her hands. "Quiet down, please."

As the murmurs in the room died down, she turned to me. "Thank you for offering, David, but I think it would be better if Jon pitched today. He's a little less...*passionate* about the game than you are."

"That works," said Cassie. Evan and Drama nodded their agreement.

I was a little disappointed at the ruling, but there was no point in arguing with the umpire. Besides, if she was going to pick someone other than me, who better than my best friend, who was also a pretty good ball player? Before heading outside, Jon and I stopped at our lockers to get our gloves.

"How long until baseball season?" Jon asked.

I didn't even have to think about the answer. "Thirty-nine days," I said as I spun the combination dial back and forth on my locker. "But you already know that."

"Yeah, but it's still fun to do the countdown with you. I guess it's because you're so *passionate* about the game."

As he emphasized Ms. Fredericks' word, he fluttered his eyelashes like he was teasing me about being in love. I wasn't in the mood for it. I grabbed my glove and slammed my locker closed.

"May as well be thirty-nine years. I'm not going to pass this science test on Monday. And when I fail for the marking period, my parents will probably kill me."

"You'll be fine," he reassured me. "Your parents are both doctors and I'm pretty sure doctors have to promise not to hurt people."

"Well, they aren't going to let me play baseball. I'm sure that'll hurt."

During our game, the score was tied for a couple of innings. My team was at bat during the bottom of the last one. I sat as patiently as I could on the bench until, finally, it was my turn to bat. Cassie was already on third base.

"You guys might want to back up," Jon said to the team on the field. "You know he's going to hit to the outfield. He always does."

Evan, Liam, and Olivia ran further into the outfield. Janie, Stella, and Jack backed up farther from the bases they were covering. Drama, who was the catcher again, relaxed behind home plate. He must've figured that, if everyone was going to be chasing the ball through the outfield, there was plenty of time before he would have to play. He stretched out his legs in front of him and crossed his hands behind his head like he was lying on the beach. I took my stance. Jon wound up and tossed the pitch. As it reached me, I switched things up. I bunted instead.

The ball hopped around near home plate. Out of the corner of my eye, I saw Drama jump up, step on the ball, lose his balance, and fall backward, shooting the ball out from under his foot. The ball bumped and hopped until it stopped inside the first base line. People scrambled in from the outfield, but it was too late. Cassie crossed home plate, and I stopped safely on first. The game was over.

CHAPTER 2

Friday, March 1 –
After School

I stood in front of my open locker and frowned at my science book. I picked it up between my thumb and forefinger like someone throwing out a dirty tissue and dropped it hastily into my backpack. Then I placed my baseball glove carefully on top of it and closed my locker door. Next to me, I heard Jon's locker close with a slam.

"Ready to go?" I asked.

He scowled at me. "You bunted?"

"We won, didn't we?"

"Yeah, but I still can't believe you bunted. That's not like you."

I shrugged my shoulders. "What can I say? I'm full of surprises today."

Jon chuckled. His anger usually melted quickly. I guess having a church deacon as a Dad made you more forgiving.

Jon and I headed down the hallway and took a left. We stopped near the second-grade classrooms to pick up my little sister Emily who stood quietly outside the classroom door. Her hair was neatly tied back in a long, dark, ponytail. Just above her clean white sneakers, she held her pink Princess Ponytail backpack so it wouldn't drag on the ground. Unlike the two girls who stood next to her, whose backpacks looked like they were dragged through the dirt on the way to school every day, Emily's backpack was still as clean and neat as the first day of school.

Jon lifted an eyebrow. "Dave, does that kid ever get dirty?"

This time I chuckled. "Once in a while, but it's rare."

I waved to get her attention. Emily swung her backpack onto her shoulders and walked toward us.

"Bye, Emily," said one of the girls standing next to her.

"Bye, Lily."

"Have a nice weekend, Emily," said the other girl.

Emily smiled. "Thanks. You, too, Sarah."

"See you Monday, Emily. Say hello to Snowball for me." A freckle-faced boy blushed a little as he talked to her.

"Bye, Ryan," said Emily. "Hope your finger feels better."

When Emily reached us, I pulled gently on the loop of her backpack to see how heavy it was. If she had a lot in it, I'd carry it for her. Today it felt light. "Hey, Emily. How was your day?" I asked.

"Not much to report," she answered, "except that Edgar bit Ryan Redmond."

"Interesting," I said. "Who's Edgar? I don't think you've mentioned him before."

"And who's Ryan Redmond?" asked Jon.

"Ryan's that kid." She leaned her head in the direction of the freckle-faced boy. I thought it was funny that she was too polite even to point at him. "And Edgar's our new class hamster. Ryan wasn't listening during science when the teacher told us how to hold him."

Sadly, I understood that problem. "Well, some kids just don't listen in science."

As we left the building, I felt the sun warming my face. "I love this weather. Why can't it be like this all the time? Then I don't have to take any lousy weather tests. Sunny and warm would be the right answer for everything."

"Right, but we need this stuff called water," said Jon. "You really don't listen in science, do you?"

A warm breeze teased Emily's ponytail by blowing some strands of her hair out of place. She didn't seem to mind, though. She was focused on something on the path ahead. Emily rushed forward. The science test was bad enough; I didn't need my little sister getting hurt on my watch.

"Careful, Emily," I said.

"I'm fine."

Emily squatted down to admire some crocuses. Their purple heads were just starting to break through the hard, brown soil. I watched as she balanced herself. She leaned forward on her toes. Her arms wrapped around the front of her knees, holding them together. Her head bent down, so her chin almost rested on her knees. With her pink backpack and jacket, she looked like a small flamingo. She smiled as she watched the flowers.

"She doesn't even get dirty when she's close to dirt," Jon said. "That's amazing."

"Our Grandma was like that, too. I remember one time when we planted seeds together. We planted them inside in cups, so they'd sprout for the summer garden. We made a huge mess in the kitchen – mud everywhere. When we were done, I needed a bath, but she never got dirty."

Jon huffed. "Your mom must have *loved* that."

"Actually, she was helping us, and she was a mess, too. Mom says she still doesn't know how Grandma stayed so clean. We laugh about it every year when we start the plants. Planting with Mom is one of the things that makes me love this time of year."

As we caught up to Emily, Jon pointed to a bird with a yellow chest and a black head. "Look at that."

"It's so pretty. What is it?" Emily asked.

If it were me answering, I just would have said it was a yellow bird, but Jon was able to be more exact.

"It's an American goldfinch," Jon answered. "Funny – it seems kind of early to see one of those."

My ears perked up again. I was hopeful. "Maybe spring's starting early?"

"Maybe, or maybe it just escaped from my Mom's ornithology lab at the University," said Jon. He made a series of short, high pitched whistles. The bird ignored him. "Guess I need to practice that one."

We watched the bird for a couple of minutes until it flew away. As we started walking again, Emily asked, "How many bird calls do you know, Jon?"

John was excited to talk about his hobby. "Only a few, but I'm pretty good at some. I can actually get mourning doves to answer."

"There are lots of baseball teams named after birds," I said.

Emily and John both stopped walking and stared at me. I stopped because they did. "What?" I asked.

"David, how do you always get us to change the subject back to baseball?" asked Emily. She shook her head and started walking again. Jon and I followed her lead.

"I think that's all Dave thinks about – baseball and spring," Jon said.

"You know it," I replied. "It'll stink if I get grounded through both. Jon, what should I do about this test?"

John shrugged. "I don't know. Right now, the only thing about weather that could help you is a snow day."

I gave him a disgusted look. "You're a big help."

John pointed at me as if telling me to wait a minute. "You never know. This is Connecticut. We get all kinds of strange weather. I mean, it's March first and look how warm it is. Who knows what'll happen next week?"

"Too bad Grandpa isn't here," said Emily. "He can teach you all you need to know about weather."

"That's if I can stay awake while he's explaining it. You'd think a weather research scientist would at least make it *interesting* to talk about the weather. Blah, blah, blah clouds...blah, blah, blah fronts..." I pretended to yawn. "A rain delay at a major league game is less boring than him."

Emily looked angry. "I love Grandpa. And I love it when he teaches me about what he's doing in the lab. Before he left on his trip, he even told me about what he's studying in Antarctica."

I rubbed her shoulders lightly to try to calm her down. "Don't get me wrong, Em," I said. "I like Grandpa – I just can't relate to him. He's kind of different and his job is weird. He goes out in all kinds of horrible weather to take 'samples'," – I made air quotes to show it was Grandpa's word – "And his lab in our basement creeps me out. It's dark and damp and full of his old junk." I shuddered at the thought of what else might live down there in the middle of all his empty jars and faded coffee mugs.

"Maybe your test wouldn't be so hard if you spent more time there," suggested Emily.

As we reached home, a three-story Victorian house, we climbed the steps to the wrap-around porch. Apart from Grandpa's creepy basement lab, I love our house. Dad had it painted sky blue with a light gray porch. Not only did this make it stand out from the rest of the boring white or brown houses on the street, but it also made our house match the colors of the Titans' baseball uniforms. That was my favorite thing about it. I knew Emily liked the small statues of garden gnomes, bunnies, turtles, and frogs standing in the planting beds around the porch and peering out from around the dormant plants. In the spring, pink azaleas, yellow and red tulips, purple crocuses, and blue and white star flowers added to the color difference between our house and the others. It was a nice change after the dirty snow colors of winter.

Another great thing about our house was that Jon and his family lived in the house's third floor apartment. When they moved in last year, it almost made up for the fact that Grandpa moved out of that apartment and moved in downstairs with our family. Mom said he did that because he was tired of cleaning and cooking just for himself.

I unlocked the front door and let Emily inside. As always, her pet cat Snowball was waiting for her. Snowball almost tripped Emily as he wove his fluffy white body back and forth between her legs, rubbing his head against her calves. The cat's long fur was neatly combed and as clean as Emily's sneakers.

Emily laughed. "Hi, Snowball. That tickles."

She set her backpack down on a small chair in the foyer, picked up Snowball, and held him like a baby. The clock on the wall above her chimed the half hour. The cat looked up at it.

"Sorry, Snowball. No tasty birdies on the half hour. The tasty cuckoo birdies only come out on the hour."

Jon frowned as he came in carrying the mail. "That's not funny, Emily. Don't encourage him to eat birds."

"He's a cat, Jon. That's what they do," I answered. See, I knew some stuff about science.

"Sorry, Jon. It's just that he likes when the cuckoo pops out." She scratched Snowball under the chin. "Maybe we should get you a kitty treat to take your mind off the cuckoo. I think Mommy bought you some chicken flavor ones for your first birthday. It's not for a couple of weeks, but I think she'd let you have one now."

"Maybe I'll buy him tuna ones instead," said Jon.

"Jon's going to buy you tasty fishy ones too," Emily said to Snowball. Snowball began to purr loudly. "Listen to that, Jon! You made him so happy."

Jon rolled his eyes. He handed me a pile of stuff he'd sorted out of the stack. "Here, Dave. This belongs to your family. A few of the letters are for your grandpa."

I took the mail from Jon. "Mom's been putting anything that's not a bill on his desk in the lab. I'll put the stuff there later, even though the place creeps me out. After all, Emily thinks I need to spend more time there." As I placed the letters on a side table near the basement door, a crazy idea hit me. "Wait...that might be the answer."

"What might be the answer?" Jon asked.

"Maybe there's something in the lab that can help me study," I answered. "Jon, want to explore with me after dinner?"

Emily frowned. "I don't think you should be in Grandpa's lab while he's away. What if you touch something you shouldn't?"

I shook my head and gave Emily a "don't be silly" wave of my hand. "Don't worry, Em, most of the stuff down there is junk. What could we possibly hurt?"

CHAPTER 3

Friday, March 1 –
Dinner

A s Jon headed upstairs, I grabbed a couple of cookies for Emily and me from the kitchen. Then I poured her a glass of milk, put on some cartoons for her to watch while she played with Snowball, and reluctantly headed to my room to study. I stood in my room, between the twin beds with half a cookie sticking out of my mouth and pulled my glove and science book out of my backpack. I tossed the backpack onto the adjacent twin bed and dropped the science book onto mine. As I finished eating my cookie, I put on my glove and punched my fist into the palm of it a few times to help me relax. "Well, old friend," I said, as I slipped it off and set it next to my backpack, "guess I'd better get busy studying or this'll be the only time I get to wear you for a while."

I flopped on my bed and opened the science book to the table of contents. There were five chapters on weather. Ugh. I flipped to the first boring chapter and began reading.

After studying for a few hours, during which time I dozed off at least twice, I learned to identify a few cloud types and memorized a couple of basic definitions. It wasn't much, but it was a start. When my stomach started growling, I realized it was time to start the next of my chores, which was setting the dinner table.

I came downstairs as the cuckoo clock in the foyer struck six. Snowball, who was curled in a ball on a kitchen chair, opened one eye to look at "the tasty birdie" before going back to sleep.

Mom and Dad were busy preparing the meal. Mom stood at the stove with a wooden spoon in her hand. Her long blonde hair was tied back in a ponytail like Emily's. Dad was standing next to her at the counter chopping vegetables for the salad. He stopped chopping when Mom popped a piece of pasta into his mouth to have him test for "done-ness". He chewed it quickly, puffing short breaths out through his teeth. "Hot, hot, hot," he gasped. Finally, Dad swallowed and gave the verdict. "Needs a couple more minutes."

Emily reached into the salad bowl and picked out a couple of carrot slices while Dad was distracted with the taste test. Mom smiled when she noticed her. "I think there's a little dark-haired mouse in your salad," Mom said.

Dad turned back to the salad. "Oh no! A mouse! Get her, Snowball!"

Snowball shifted his ears slightly in Dad's direction, but otherwise kept his eyes closed. "Some mouser you are," said Dad. "Guess I'll just have to take care of her myself."

Dad wrapped his arms around Emily in a big bear hug and lifted her off the ground. Emily giggled as she popped the last of her stolen carrots into her mouth. "Too late," she said.

"And I thought I had you that time." Dad gave her a kiss on the cheek and set her down.

Just as it was rare for Emily to get dirty, it was also strange to have both of my parents home for a weeknight dinner. On the nights when Mom worked the evening shift at the hospital, Dad came home to cook. And, if Mom had a night at home, Dad usually had administrative meetings, patient rounds, or other work stuff until it was almost Emily's bedtime. Dad always joked that the busy schedule of a hospital administrator was adding streaks of gray to his jet-black hair. Mom would laugh and suggest that it was thinning it out, too.

But, tonight, the whole family dinner was going to be quick. In about an hour, Mom and Dad were taking Emily to see the latest Princess Ponytail movie. This was a good thing because there would be less time for my parents to ask about my day. Hopefully I could avoid the subject of the test I was going to fail.

I took the plates out of the cabinet and set the pile on the table. Mom looked at me with concern. "Were you in your room, David?"

I did the dashboard ornament nod again.

"That's the last place I'd expect to find you on a beautiful Friday afternoon. Are you sick?" she asked.

Mom and Dad came over to me. She reached for my forehead as he reached for my wrist and took my pulse. Emily laughed.

"Practicing your bedside humor again?" I asked.

"Sorry, son, force of habit. But, seriously, how are you feeling? You never miss an opportunity to be on the ball field at Fairlane Park," said Dad.

"I'm fine. I've just got a lot of studying to do." I hoped that would be the end of their questions.

"He's got a big science test on Monday," said Emily.

Thankfully, that was all she shared about my test.

"Guess that means we won't be able to have our annual car wash day this weekend," said Dad. I shook my head no. "No worries. It can wait another week. Besides, it might be early to start washing all the winter salt off the cars. We may still get snow this season."

I was glad that Dad was willing to wait. Helping him wash the cars was one of the other things I loved to do each year when the weather started to get warm. It gave us some one-on-one time. And as far as his snow prediction was concerned, I thought Sunday night would be a great time for it to come true and delay the big test.

"Well, anyway, I'm glad to see you taking your studies so seriously, especially science," Dad said. "Sometimes I worry you're only focused on baseball at this time of year."

"You guys always tell me to keep my priorities straight," I said as I tried to evade the question. I felt my face start to flush from not being totally honest, so I hurried to finish setting the table. At this rate, the sooner this dinner was over, the better. I did my best to keep things moving. "Look at the time. We should eat. You've got a movie to catch. Right, Em?"

"No rush, pal. We have some time," said Dad, "and a little surprise."

I wasn't sure I wanted any more surprises today. "You do?"

"Yes, David. Mom and I were talking the other day about what a big help you've been, especially with both of us working so much. You've brought Emily to and from school every day. You've been helping around the house. You've even helped shovel snow."

"We know how you hate shoveling snow," said Mom.

I nodded in agreement. I was glad there was a piece of our conversation where I could be truthful.

"Well," Dad continued, "we have a special reward for you for all your hard work."

"It's also an incentive to keep you working hard through these last few months of school," Mom added.

"What is it?" Emily asked.

Dad grinned from ear to ear. "We bought tickets for all of us to go to every Titans home game this summer."

My mouth dropped open. "You what?"

"We were going to wait a couple of weeks until your grades came out," said Mom, "but, Dad and I both feel confident that you're going to do well. Surprise!" She gave me a side hug with the arm that wasn't holding the pasta stirring spoon. Emily clapped happily.

On any other day, I would have been jumping out of my cleats at getting Titans tickets. But, today, this news felt like a punch in the gut. Losing the tickets because of this dumb test was too much to take. And, I *would* lose the tickets when I failed.

Mom gave me another squeeze when I didn't answer. "I think he might actually be speechless."

I tried to think fast. "Are you guys sure? I mean those tickets are expensive."

"Don't worry about that. We just want you to know how proud we are of you," said Dad.

I forced myself to smile and to look excited so they wouldn't suspect anything. "Wow. Thanks. I didn't realize you had so much confidence in me."

"Of course, we do. We love you, David," said Mom.

"I love you guys too," I said.

I hoped all that pride and love would soften their punishment when they saw the big "F" on my report card.

Mom went back to the stove and then to the sink to drain the pasta.

"Is Grandpa coming to the games with us?" asked Emily.

"Absolutely." Dad set the salad bowl on the table. "We're taking the whole family. Well, except for Snowball. I'm sure they don't allow cats into the stadium."

Emily's kitty uncurled himself from his nap, stretched out his paws and gave a yawn. He blinked at Dad as if to say, "What makes you think I'm interested in going with you? I clearly have more important things to do – like sleeping."

As we sat down to eat, I thought that Snowball might be a better choice to take to the game than Grandpa. At least the cat knew how to chase a ball, which was probably more than Grandpa knew about the sport. Whenever Grandpa came to one of my games, he usually wound up staring wistfully into the sky like he was watching the weather more than the game. But, no, Grandpa would be going to the Titans games while I was grounded. It just didn't seem right. Then again, there was the possibility that Grandpa could pull me out of this mess. I kept my fingers crossed that the lab held an answer.

CHAPTER 4

Friday, March 1 – After Dinner

"You're right, Dave," said Jon as we entered the lab. "This place is strange."

"It's home sweet home to Grandpa, if that tells you anything."

I walked to Grandpa's desk and added the letters to the already teetering pile. The mail was threatening to overflow its basket, slide over the side of the desk, and land in a spider web that stretched between the desk leg and the wall. I tried to adjust the stack so it wouldn't fall. No spider deserved that.

"I'm surprised Emily will come down here," said Jon. "Looks too messy for her."

"Actually," I said, "the lab is usually pretty clean. It's just getting dusty because Grandpa's been gone for two months. But I think Emily might still come down here if it were messy. She and Grandpa are pretty close."

"When's he coming back?"

"Late next week, I think."

The pile of mail toppled over. Most of it stayed on the desk, but a few pieces landed in the spider web. Sorry, spider. I tried.

Jon looked quickly around the rest of the room. "Well, I can see why you wouldn't want to be down here. You like the sunshine too much."

"I used to like it down here when I was small, but then..."

As I stared at the long, heavy, black-topped wooden table that stood in the center of the room, my mind flashed back to my last memories of spending any real time here with Grandpa. I was about five. I thought about how excited Grandpa was at dinner the night before...

"I'll bet I can change the color of the snow by dyeing the marshmallows like Easter eggs," said Grandpa.

"Won't all those colors just turn the snow black when they mix?" Grandma asked. She began clearing the dirty plates from the table.

"Sounds depressing," said Mom. She was feeding a bottle to Emily.

Dad added his opinion. "What difference would it make? Snow gets dirty after a couple of days anyway."

"Don't listen to the naysayers, David," said Grandpa. "You want to help me dye marshmallows like Easter eggs tomorrow, don't you?"

I nodded enthusiastically. I had no idea what Grandpa meant about the snow, but coloring marshmallows sounded fun. So, the next day, I sat on one of the stools next to the black-topped table. I remembered swinging my legs back and forth as Grandpa showed me what to do.

"I want you to take the marshmallows like this." Grandpa picked one up with some tweezers. "Then you're going to put it into whatever color you want until the marshmallow changes color. You can even do them half one color and half another if you want."

I nodded.

"See, just put it on its side like this." He showed me how to stand it on end in the dye so only half would change color. After about a minute, he took it out of the dye and set it on a wire rack to dry. "Got it?"

"Mm-hmm," I said.

"Good. Oh, and you can eat a few, too, if you want." Grandpa gave me a wink, popped a marshmallow in his mouth, and went to work on other things.

At first, I watched him scurry around the lab. Grandpa checked the thermometers and other equipment with dials that covered the open wall space. Then, he flipped through the paper graphs that were spread out on his desk. He never trusted computers, so there were neat stacks of paper in piles surrounding his desk that he kept stepping around. Then he hurried to the shelves along the walls that were lined with old textbooks, empty jars, and chipped coffee mugs and he changed the music from one Christmas Carol to another on something he called a record player.

I turned back to the marshmallows. Grandpa had six dishes with different colored dyes in them. He'd also set the marshmallows out in piles of six – one for each color of dye. I took care of one pile by standing one marshmallow in each of the six dishes. I stood each one, so half the marshmallow was in the dye and half was out, like he showed me. Then I took care of another pile by eating the six marshmallows. When the ones in the dye looked good on one side, I flipped them over and put the still white half in another color. I didn't think much about the color combinations except for making sure that the last one was half red and half green for Christmas. I did that one for Grandma because I knew how much she liked Christmas. Then I ate six more marshmallows – one for each one I flipped. When the ones in the dye were done, I took them out and set them on the rack to dry. I ate one undyed marshmallow each time I took a finished one out of the dishes. I was just about to take the red and green one out when Grandma came in.

"I'm heading to work soon. Just wanted to see how you're doing," said Grandma.

"Look, Grandma!" I held up the red and green marshmallow for her to see.

"That's pretty, David," she said. "Looks like Christmas."

I got so excited that she liked it, that I accidentally dropped it. It splashed into the purple dye and started turning a deep purple-black color. I started to cry because I ruined Grandma's marshmallow and my stomach was starting to hurt. They both came over to see what was wrong.

"I guess you were right, dear," said Grandpa as he saw the dropped marshmallow. "It does turn black."

Grandpa and Grandma took me upstairs, washed me up, and tucked me into bed. Then Grandma kissed both Grandpa and me and headed off to work.

Later that day when I was lying in bed, my mom came in to check on me. Her eyes were red and puffy. I thought she was upset because I wasn't feeling well.

"Mommy, please don't cry. I won't eat any more marshmallows."

"I'm not upset about that, honey," she answered. "I'm upset because Grandma had an accident."

I overheard my parents talking about it later that night. Grandma's car slid on a patch of ice while she was on her way to work as a manager at a local inn. She wasn't going that fast, but the car hit a tree at an odd angle and Grandma was severely hurt. She died at the hospital not long after arriving there. On the car seat next to her was a bag of groceries mostly for the kitchen at the inn, but it also included a bag of marshmallows for Grandpa's experiment to replace the one's I'd eaten. After that day, I always felt queasy at the sight of marshmallows, and I stopped spending time in the lab. Clearly, these events were the catalyst for my dislike of marshmallows, weather science, and winter.

"Hey, what's this thing?" Jon's voice snapped me back to real time.

He was standing next to something I'd seen before, but never actually saw Grandpa use. I didn't know its purpose. It was a six-foot-tall, narrow, freestanding case with metal edges, a metal top and bottom, and glass walls. It was completely enclosed except for a small, sliding door in the front at the bottom and a drain in the center of the base. I would have said it was a shower stall, but the door wasn't even big enough for Snowball to go through and there was no showerhead.

"Jon, I have no idea what that is, and I'm not sure I want to know."

"Looks like a weird, see-through school locker with a really tiny door." said Jon. "Weren't you even curious about it?"

I huffed. "Sure, Jon. I wondered every day because I'm always so interested in science. Can we move along now?"

Jon walked over to some bookcases. "So, where do you want to start looking?"

"You can start wherever you want. I think I'm going to look in his notebooks first. Maybe he'll have things explained in a way I can understand."

I flipped through some notebooks I found on one of Grandpa's shelves. They looked more confusing than the charts on the school chalkboard. Jon took some other books off the shelves, but he didn't find anything useful either. It didn't take long for me to surrender.

"This isn't going to help me. Let's put everything back and use our own books. Maybe, if I don't sleep for the next two days, I can still squeeze out a 'D' on the test."

Jon closed the book he was reading. "I still think you should start praying for a snow day."

"Since your dad's a deacon, I'll leave that to you," I answered. "My family's more the scientific type."

Jon raised an eyebrow. "And how's that working for you?"

I groaned and picked up a stack of books and notebooks. The shelf shook as I dropped them on it with a loud "thud". From the topmost shelf, a small, soft bag and some dust fell on my head. Jon sneezed.

"I should have worn my batting helmet in here," I mumbled as I brushed the dust from my hair.

When I picked up the bag, I noticed printing on it. It said, "Snowmallows – Put two in your evening hot cocoa and it will snow measurably for two days." The bag had more writing on it, but I was too excited to bother reading any more.

"Jon, check this out. It's exactly what I need. Grandpa's giving me a snow day!"

CHAPTER 5

Friday, March 1 – Early Evening

We rushed from the lab straight to the kitchen. I opened the cabinet and grabbed the cocoa powder, sugar, and salt.

"What are you doing?" asked Jon.

I thought what I was doing was obvious. "Making cocoa." My words escaped my mouth in a tone that sounded more like a question than a statement.

"When I make cocoa, I open the package and pour in the hot water."

Now I saw the problem. "You mean instant? Grandpa and Mom hate that stuff. They insist on making it from scratch."

I mixed the dry ingredients in water and put them on the stove to boil. I stirred them until it was time to add the milk.

Jon glanced cautiously at the Snowmallow bag. "Are you sure it's a good idea to use these things?"

"Sure, why not?"

"Well, it's not like we asked permission to be in the lab. You sure we're not going to get in trouble?"

"I'm allowed to go in the lab," I said stubbornly. "I don't need to ask permission."

"Yes, Dave, but you've also never seen Dr. Wilson – I mean your grandpa – use these. Until today, you didn't know they existed. What if they're not safe?"

I huffed impatiently. I knew what was bothering him. "Stop worrying, Jon. We're not going to hurt your 'good kid' reputation."

"That's not it. I just think we should be careful," said Jon.

"Relax," I answered. "Grandpa's got to have an antidote in the lab if we need it. I don't think he'd keep these if he didn't."

When the cocoa was done, I poured it into two mugs and we headed for the front porch. I set the full mugs on the porch railing while we talked about what to do next.

"Let's see," I thought out loud. "It's Friday night. So, if we use two Snowmallows each, we'll have four days of snow. That should cancel school until Wednesday, at least."

"Then, if you need more time off, I guess we'll just use more Snowmallows," said Jon.

"That's the spirit," I said.

Cautiously, I opened the bag. A whoosh of air floated up from it, filling my nose with the scent of burnt wood. It was so strong, it made me cough. I reached into the bag to take out four Snowmallows. Each one was white. They looked like they were supposed to be shaped like snowflakes, but they were slightly soggy and sticky between my fingers – a lot like melting marshmallows – so they came out in a sort of clump. I separated out what looked like four and I paused. The feel of them on my fingers made my stomach churn. The last time I mixed science and marshmallows was one of the worst days of my life. Maybe Jon was right to worry, but this was the only option. I had to pass that test. All I could hope was that history wouldn't repeat itself.

"Well, here goes nothin'." I scraped them off my fingers with a spoon, plopping two goopy blobs into each mug.

Jon shuddered. "That's disgusting." I couldn't argue with him.

The Snowmallows floated lazily on top of the cocoa as Jon and I stared at the mugs. Part of me was excited. Another part of me was scared. But, after waiting for what seemed like forever, nothing happened. Then I was just disappointed. We had to be doing something wrong, but what?

"I guess...we're supposed to, um, drink it?" I suggested. I really hoped that wasn't the answer.

Jon made a gagging, sound. "Seriously? Um, No!"

Suddenly, the Snowmallows began to fizz. They turned the cocoa into frothy brown foam that sputtered and oozed over the side of each mug. We jumped back so none of the gook would land on us. It looked like a super-charged ice cream soda. Crash! The slimy coating shattered the mugs into dusty pieces. The whole mixture fizzed a few more seconds. Then it evaporated in sparkles like fireflies flickering up into the sky. The words to "Silent Night" whispered through the air. No trace of the mixture was left anywhere on the porch. As we looked out into the darkness, light, fluffy snowflakes like small clumps of cotton candy began to fall. Both of us were speechless for a minute.

I was so stunned I said the first thing that came into my head. "Do you think that's why Grandpa has so many old mugs?"

Jon's eyes widened. "That's what you think of when that stuff explodes? I'm just glad you didn't convince me to drink it."

CHAPTER 6

Tuesday, March 5 – After Dinner

The next morning, the ground was covered in a blanket of white. A powdery snow continued to fall throughout the rest of the weekend. It snowed on Monday and Tuesday, too, so school was closed both days. By Tuesday night, there was a ridiculous amount of snow on the ground – at least thirty inches – so the Snowmallows worked great.

I didn't waste the opportunity that Grandpa's invention gave me. I studied, outlined, and memorized the weather information in my book, usually until late in the evening each night. Unfortunately, all that work didn't excuse me from having to go outside to shovel the front walks and the driveway during the storm. The hospital needed Dad, so while he was at work, I had to keep things clear. I needed the snow days, but I still hated shoveling. I was glad that Jon and his dad, Deacon Strong, were around and willing to help me. And, in the end, a couple of rounds of shoveling was a small price to pay to save baseball season.

By Tuesday evening, I felt ready for the test. I was also done studying early enough that I could relax for a little while before bed. I headed downstairs to the living room to watch some TV with Mom and Emily. I expected it to be calm – a time to wind down – but, when I went downstairs, the living room wasn't quiet at all. It was full of activity.

"What's going on?" I asked.

"Hi, honey," said Mom. She was stuffing clothes from the clean laundry basket into two backpacks. "I was just coming upstairs to see you. Your dad called from the hospital. He said that a lot of our co-workers can't get in because of the snow. They need my help there, so he's sending a security vehicle to pick me up. I'm leaving soon."

Emily sat on the floor shaking a colorful feather toy in front of Snowball. Snowball batted it with his paws and nipped at the tip of the feather with his teeth. "How long will you be gone, Mommy?" Emily asked.

"I don't know, baby. Not long, I hope, but that depends on the storm." Mom went into her bathroom and came back with her toothbrush, Dad's toothbrush, and some toothpaste that she threw into the side pocket of one of the backpacks. "I hate to leave the two of you, but I think David's responsible enough to handle things here for a little while."

Mom's trust in me made me uneasy, especially since I was the reason it was snowing in the first place, but I knew things were going as planned.

"Besides, the snow will stop soon," I said.

"That'd be nice, but no one knows for sure," answered Mom. "I was just watching the news, and Brian the Meteorologist said it looks like the storm may be getting worse. School's already cancelled for tomorrow."

Emily stopped playing with Snowball and gave Mom a worried look. "How long are you going to stay at work? What if it keeps snowing and you have to be there for days?"

Mom placed the last items in the backpacks and zipped them up. Then she sat on the floor next to Emily and stroked her hair. "I don't expect that to happen, but I don't know for sure. Just in case, I called upstairs to let Deacon and Mrs. Strong know that Dad and I are needed at work. They'll check in on you tomorrow and they'll help you with anything that comes up. Mrs. Strong even invited you to stay with them tonight, but I told her I thought you'd be happier sleeping in your own beds." Mom looked up at me. "Now, David, there's plenty of food for both of you in the pantry and fridge, and I just bought more food for Snowball, so you should be fine."

A car horn beeped outside.

"There's my ride." Mom hugged and kissed Emily. Then she stood up and hugged and kissed me. "You two be careful and watch out for one another. I have my cell phone, so I'll check in periodically. I love you."

Emily and I responded together. "We love you, too."

With that, Mom buttoned her coat, grabbed the two backpacks, and headed out the door. As she waved to us through the window of the security vehicle, I tried to reassure myself that the snow was stopping soon.

CHAPTER 7

Wednesday, March 6 – Morning

Emily and I both slept in on Wednesday. It was nice to have at least one snow day to forget about school. I figured this day off would be what Mom and Dad called a "wasted snow day" – a day where school was cancelled because everyone expected a big storm and then nothing came. But, when I woke up, the sky was still covered with gloomy, gray-white clouds that were spitting heavy snow in every direction. The wind was gusting, too. It blew the falling snow into swirls that looked like the tops of soft serve ice cream cones. The snow drifts were piled high against the front doors of the houses across the street so that only the top third of each door was uncovered. I hoped the neighbors could get out through the back. Then I thought for a minute. Something didn't seem right. I started counting the days off on my fingers. Saturday, Sunday, Monday, Tuesday makes four days. The snow should have stopped by now. Goosebumps pricked my arms.

I went to the kitchen and found Emily pouring some Crunchy Salmon Bits into Snowball's dish.

"When did you get up?" I asked her.

She rubbed her eyes and yawned. "A few minutes ago. Snowball jumped on my bed and stuck his whiskers in my face. I guess he got tired of waiting for breakfast."

"Well, I'm hungry, too. Should we join him?"

Another yawn. "I guess. Grandpa always says it's no fun eating alone."

I poured cereal for Emily and me for breakfast and turned on the kitchen television. It was still on the channel Mom was watching last night. There was a special extended news broadcast because of the storm.

"Can we watch cartoons?" asked Emily.

"Sure."

I was about to change the channel, but I didn't. The news people were showing some unsettling pictures of the storm.

"Larry, look at these pictures sent in by our viewers," said one news anchor to the other.

"They are amazing, Carla!" said Larry. "Here's one of a car buried in a snowbank. The viewer writes that the only reason he saw it was because the emergency flashers were still blinking through the snow. I wonder how long those flashers will last!"

"And look at this. These poor children are looking longingly out the window. Their mom emailed that they want to go outside and play in the snow so badly, but it's too deep for them. She's afraid she'll lose them out there," Carla added.

"Well, here's some footage from right outside our studios. Many walkways are still impassible, so these people seem to be wading through the snow by finding places where it's only knee deep. Wherever they're going, it's got to be hard to see with the snow coming down so heavily. I don't know about you, Carla, but I'm glad I'm not out there!"

"I agree, Larry. And to find out more about what's going on out there, let's stay in here and talk to our meteorologist, Brian, in the weather center. Hi, Brian, what's causing all this crazy weather?"

"Thanks, Larry and Carla. Well, I hate to admit it, but I have no explanation for what's caused this sudden change to severe winter conditions around the city," said Brian the Meteorologist. "And it looks like things are just going to get worse. It's like all the weather models we looked at earlier this week took a complete 180-degree turn..."

You mean they took a Snowmallow swerve, I thought.

"Hey, David, I thought we were going to watch cartoons," Emily complained.

I handed her the TV clicker and scarfed down my cereal. "When you're done with breakfast, put your dish in the sink and get dressed," I told her. "I'm going to get dressed and go upstairs to see Jon. I'll be back."

"Mm-hmm," she said through a mouthful of Fruity O's while she stared at Princess Ponytail on the TV.

I took the stairs two at a time, and when I reached the top, Jon answered the door.

"Jon, I think we messed up somewhere."

"Well, good morning to you, too," Jon said.

"Sorry. No time for pleasantries. Why is it still snowing? It should've stopped last night."

Jon shook his head. "Maybe this isn't because of the Snowmallows."

I couldn't believe my ears. "How can you think it's not the Snowmallows? The day we used them it was sixty-five degrees and sunny. Now we've had about four feet of snow in four days. Even Brian, the TV meteorologist, doesn't know why this is happening. At this rate, we could be snowed in for months! Baseball season may never come!"

Jon put his hand up in a motion that said stop. "Dave, take a breath."

I paused, took a deep breath, and let it out again. It helped me feel calmer but didn't solve my problem. I had to make Jon understand. "Jon, you saw what they did when we put them in the cocoa. This must be the Snowmallows. We started this and we need to stop it. Let's look in the lab again to see what we can find."

* * *

In the lab, we looked up at the top shelf of the bookcase where we'd tossed the Snowmallow bag on Friday after we were done with it. We tried shaking the shelf again to get the bag down, but it was too far back to fall off this time.

"How are we getting it down? Does your Grandpa have a ladder or something down here?" asked Jon.

"I think so, but I don't know where exactly. Let's try this instead."

I grabbed one of Grandpa's golf umbrellas. I tapped the tip of the umbrella against the bottom of the shelf. The shelf tilted enough for the bag to slide off. Unfortunately, a notebook and a small pile of dust slid off, too. All of it landed on Jon. His dark hair and glasses were covered in a thin gray film.

"Puh!" Jon puffed some dust away from his mouth. He sneezed twice. "Thanks for the shower."

"Sorry, Jon. Here, wash off in the sink."

Jon handed me the bag and the notebook that he skillfully caught through the dust storm and went to the sink. In between sneezes, he cleaned his glasses and brushed off his hair while I re-read the Snowmallow bag. I saw writing on it that I didn't notice before.

"Uh Oh," I said.

"What's wrong?" The voice was not Jon's and it startled me.

"Emily, don't scare me like that!"

She came into the lab with Snowball following her. Emily stared at the bag in my hand. "You found the Snowmallows?"

I frowned at her. "How do you know what these are?"

She put her hands on her hips and tilted her head to one side. "I'm the one who spends time in the lab with Grandpa, remember?"

At least she was nice enough not to add the word "Duh" when she said it. I felt stupid enough already. "Point taken," I said.

She continued. "The other day, when I heard you talking about snow days and searching the lab, I tried to hide them. Did you use them?"

This time it was my turn not to say "Duh". "Look outside, Emily. What do you think?"

Jon came over. He was wiping his hair with wet paper towels. "Forgive me," he said, "I may have dust in my ears, but I thought I heard Little Miss Clean Sneakers say she hid the Snowmallows way up there with all the dirt."

Emily nodded.

My big brother instinct kicked in. I didn't need another problem, like a sister with a broken wrist, on my hands. "You climbed way up there?"

"No. I threw them. You guys aren't the only ones who can throw stuff, you know," Emily said.

My anger melted. "Wow," I said. "Good arm. I can teach you a couple of pitches if you want."

"Hello," said Jon. "Remember the snow? Focus, please."

"Sorry. You're right. And, we have a bigger problem." I showed Jon the bag.

"Uh Oh," he said.

"Why does everyone keep saying that?" Emily asked.

I read her the writing on the bag that I noticed when she came in. "WARNING: Do not use more than two Snowmallows per day. Results of tests showed unpredictable weather beyond that limit."

"So?" said Emily.

I sighed. "So, we used four."

"Uh oh," said Emily.

"It'll be fine, though, Em. Since you know about Grandpa's work with them, you can tell us how to stop them."

She shook her head from side to side so her ponytail brushed her shoulders. "I don't know how to stop them. I don't think Grandpa ever made a formula for that."

I couldn't believe it. "What? Why not?"

She shrugged her shoulders. "I don't know. Maybe it's because he usually only uses them on Christmas Eve. And, he never uses them outside the weather locker." She pointed to the metal and glass contraption in the corner. "He says they're 'safely contained' in there. They stop on their own when the cloud runs out of water."

"Do you know if he's ever started to work on a formula?" asked Jon.

"I don't know about that, either. But, in Antarctica, he's working on ways to make winter storms not as bad." She smiled optimistically. "Maybe he'll have the answer when he gets back."

My face suddenly felt clammy. Not only had I unleashed the Snowmallows outside the lab and changed the weather, but now I had no way to change it back.

CHAPTER 8

Wednesday, March 6 – Mid-Morning

"Em, we have to try to fix what happened," I said. "You need to tell us all you know about the Snowmallows."

Emily smiled like there was nothing to worry about. "Grandpa's coming home tomorrow. Let's wait for him. He'll fix it."

Jon rubbed his forehead with the tips of his fingers. "But, Emily, your Grandpa won't be able to get home. I saw on TV this morning that no planes are flying in or out of the airport because of all the snow."

"And if it keeps snowing this way, it could be weeks until the planes fly again," I added.

Her smile immediately disappeared. "Can't we call him or something?"

I put my hand softly on her shoulder. "Even if he's someplace where he has cell service – which is a big if – what are we going to tell him? Do you think he'll be happy we've been messing with the stuff in his lab?" She didn't answer me. "We have to do this ourselves, Em. You need to tell us what you know about the Snowmallows. It's the only way."

Emily sat down on one of the stools near the black topped table. Her body sank down like she was wearing a backpack full of boulders. Snowball jumped into her lap. She petted the cat as she thought hard about what to do. Snowball was starting to shed his winter coat, so small clumps of loose fur brushed off him and floated into the air with each stroke of Emily's hand. Jon sneezed as a ball of fluff sailed past him.

"Emily, I'm allergic to cat hair. Can you please stop petting him?" He covered his nose with the paper towel he'd used to dry his glasses.

"Sorry. Petting Snowball helps me think."

Jon sneezed again. "Then can you think a little faster?"

"All right," said Emily. "I'll help, but I don't understand all of it."

"Don't worry about it, Em. Anything you tell us will be more than we know now," I said.

"Well, what do you know?" she asked.

I shrugged. "Nothing."

Jon smiled. "That's why what you tell us will be more than what we know."

Emily rolled her eyes and set Snowball down on the floor. She got a pencil from Grandpa's desk and sat down at the table again. Then she took Grandpa's notebook from me and flipped to a blank page.

"I'll show you like Grandpa showed me."

She drew a curved line, like a frown, at the bottom of the page. "This is the Earth."

I could tell how tense she was, so I tried joking with her. "No, Em. If you're going to tell it like Grandpa, then you need to do the looking over the glasses thing that he does."

Emily's was still looking down at the paper. When I made my joke, she turned her head slightly to the right and lifted her eyes to look at me. "What?" she asked.

"Yeah, that's it. That's the look," I said. "Only your head needs to be straighter, not tilted to the right like that. And you need to scrunch up your lips more. Like this." I pursed my lips slightly. "Then you'll look just like him."

Emily raised an eyebrow. I could tell she was not amused. "If you're going to pick on Grandpa, I'm not going to help you."

"Take it easy. I was just trying to lighten the mood to help you think better."

Emily frowned at me. Apparently, my plan wasn't working. "Never mind, Em. Keep going. I'm listening."

Emily turned her head back to the paper. "As I was saying, this curved line is the Earth."

Above the curved line, she drew two straight horizontal lines, one above the other. "This is the air around the earth. It's in layers." Next, she drew an arrow going up from the Earth through the layers of air. "As you go up each layer, the air gets colder."

Jon and I nodded. So far, we knew what she was talking about.

Then she drew a down arrow next to the up arrow. "But, the Snowmallows make that go backward. So, it's colder on the ground and warmer higher up."

"That's called temperature inversion," said Jon. "It was in our science book."

Emily drew a sun on the right side of the picture. "Grandpa said that the sun comes up in the east." She drew a cloud on the left side of the picture. "But the weather comes from the west. The Snowmallows change that, too, so the weather comes from the same direction as the sun."

I thought out loud. "That means that now...the clouds are coming from over the ocean. That's why we're getting so much snow – the clouds are full of moisture from the ocean." I felt happy that what I studied made sense to me. Maybe I would pass my test – if I ever got to take it.

"But what's in the Snowmallows that makes that happen?" Jon asked.

"There's a formula for them in here," said Emily. She flipped to another page in the notebook and handed it to me. I read the formula to them.

Snowmallows	
1 jar	Cold blizzard wind that has just whistled through the trees
1/4 cup	Ashes taken from fireplace after first burnt log of the season
1/8 cup	Ice shavings wiped from skates after ice-skating on Milton's Pond
1 jar	Christmas Carols sung door to door
1 tsp	Charcoal dust from snowman's eyes
1 bag	Marshmallows - 12 ounces

"What kind of crazy stuff is that?" asked Jon.

Emily smiled. "Grandpa said that Snowmallows are the best things about winter put together."

I scratched my head. "But how does he make them? Where's he get all those things?"

"I saw him make them once." Emily pointed to the shelves along the wall. "Grandpa has most of the winter things in those jars, except the ice shavings. Those are in the old freezer near the sink."

I glanced around the lab. The jars on the shelves weren't empty. They filled with invisible things like Christmas Carols and blizzard winds.

"Have you ever seen him use the Snowmallows?" asked Jon.

"Yes. When he wants to use them, he puts a mug of cocoa in the weather locker, adds the Snowmallows to it, and watches through the glass to see what happens."

I looked back at the notebook. Grandpa had notes below the formula.

"Listen to this," I said. I began reading again.

Snowmallow ingredients turn calm weather to snowy weather in minutes:

1 Reaction begins when Snowmallows are added to hot cocoa.
2 Hot cocoa provides liquid to form clouds.
3 Charcoal dust provides particles for water in clouds to attach to, making it heavy enough to fall as precipitation.
4 Temperature inversion occurs when ashes from fireplace help heat from cocoa to rise.

5 Ice shavings assist temperature inversion by helping ground stay colder – also keep snow from melting on ground contact.
6 Blizzard wind changes the weather direction to East-West flow and assists with Nor'Easter storm conditions.
7 Christmas Carols, cheerful sounds of the season, give hope, acting as a catalyst for the mixture to work.
8 Marshmallows hold ingredients together, so they are added evenly to cocoa, but have no chemically reactive properties in the formula.

All of us sat quietly for a couple of minutes. I was pretty sure that meant that none of us knew what to do next.

CHAPTER 9

Wednesday, March 6 – Lunch

"**J**on? David? Emily? Where are you?" Mrs. Theresa Strong, Jon's mom, who everyone called Tess, summoned us from the top of the stairs. "Do you guys want some lunch?"

I sighed softly. "Come on, let's go upstairs. I don't want your parents to find out what we did."

"What do you mean *we*?" asked Emily.

I nodded. As much as I hated to admit it, I'd started this mess.

Jon, Emily, Snowball, and I climbed the stairs to the third floor.

"Snowball should stay out here, Em," I said. "Jon doesn't need all that fur in his house."

"Stay here, Snowball. I'll be right back," said Emily.

We went inside and closed the door, but Snowball kept crying from the other side of the door. Mrs. Strong made a sad face and put her hand over her heart. "Let him in. I'll vacuum later. Jon will be fine."

Snowball happily hopped across the threshold when we opened the door and followed us into the Strong's small kitchen, sniffing everything he passed. Jon's dad, Deacon Mike Strong, was in the living room watching TV. Normally, he was cheerful. But, today, he sat leaning forward on the sofa with his elbows on his knees. His hands were folded against his face with his pointer fingers under his nose and his thumbs under his chin. The brow behind his wire rimmed glasses was furrowed as he watched the latest snow reports on the news. I couldn't tell if he was thinking or praying, but I didn't want to disturb him.

Mrs. Strong set ham and cheese sandwiches in front of each of our places at the table. She had a well-worn apron on over her long-sleeved t-shirt and jeans as she bustled about the kitchen. Her energy always amazed me. I don't think I ever saw her sit for more than ten minutes at a time. According to Jon, if she wasn't rushing around at the University, she was usually on her feet in the kitchen cooking or baking something. Deacon Strong often joked that she kept "his belly well-rounded", but I knew that a lot of what she made was for other people. I once helped Jon deliver a dish of baked ziti to the Connells across the street when they had their new baby. And we brought a plate of cookies next door to ninety-year-old Molly Fischer when her great-grandchildren came to visit at Christmastime. That was what I liked about Jon's mom – no matter how busy she was, she always found little ways to show people that she was thinking of them.

Mrs. Strong walked over to the sofa and gently laid her hand on her husband's shoulder. His focus shifted to her. "Time for lunch?" he asked. She nodded.

Deacon Strong turned off the television. "Tess, please remind me to give Molly Fischer a call this afternoon. I want to make sure she has what she needs." He walked to the kitchen table and sat down.

Mrs. Strong sat down, too. Just for fun, I glanced at the clock on the wall to see how long she'd stay that way. "Good idea," she said. "Molly's always so happy to hear from you."

Deacon Strong turned to the rest of us. "Ready for prayer?"

Emily, who already had her sandwich in her hand and was about to take a bite of it, gave me a confused look. I knew from past visits that Jon's family always prayed before meals, but she wasn't used to it. I bowed my head to let her know to do the same. She bowed her head but kept holding the sandwich.

Deacon Strong led us. "Lord, please bless this food we are about to share. We thank you for it and for all your many blessings. Amen."

"Amen," said Mrs. Strong and Jon.

When everyone stopped talking, Emily lifted her head slightly to see if she was clear to eat. I nodded, so she finally took a bite.

"So, what've you kids been up to this morning?" Deacon Strong asked.

"Nothin'," Jon answered.

"That doesn't sound like much fun," said Deacon Strong.

Mrs. Strong looked down at Snowball. He sat at the corner of the table between Deacon and Mrs. Strong's chairs and looked up at them like he was hoping for a handout. "Maybe you should ask this attentive looking cat over here. He looks pretty happy, so he must have had a fun morning."

"What's the good word, Snowball?" asked Deacon Strong. Snowball stared up at him and licked his mouth. He slowly lifted the heels of his paws up and down and opened and closed his toes. Then Snowball started to purr. "You're right, Tess. He does seem happy. Must be because he's so clean and white. How does he stay so well groomed, Emily?"

"You think he's clean, check out Emily's sneakers," said Jon.

Emily was sitting on the other side of Deacon Strong, so he peeked under the table at her shoes. "Very nice. Are they new, Emily?"

"They were new in September," she said.

The Deacon looked surprised. "That's impressive. Maybe you guys really didn't do anything this morning. Emily's shoes didn't even get dirty."

Snowball softly meowed once as if reminding us he was there. Deacon Strong leaned closer to Emily. "Is Snowball allowed table scraps?" he whispered.

Emily nodded.

The Deacon sat straight again. Mrs. Strong eyed him suspiciously. "You're plotting something. I can tell," she said.

"Who? Me?" he said. "Never. Oh, by the way, may I please have a napkin?"

When Mrs. Strong turned toward Jon to reach the napkin holder, Deacon Strong slipped a bite of ham to Snowball. He gave us a sneaky smile. Emily stifled a giggle.

"You know I saw that, right?" Mrs. Strong said as she handed him a napkin.

"Snagged," said the Deacon.

This time Emily couldn't stop her laugh.

Mrs. Strong passed out napkins to the rest of us. "Now, Mike, let's get back to your original question. Of course, they stayed clean. What could any of them do to get dirty when they're stuck inside in the middle of this storm?" Jon gave me a knowing smile and brushed a little pretend dust off his sleeve.

"You're right." Deacon Strong nodded. "This is some storm. Isn't it, guys?"

"Yup, some storm," I agreed.

"I don't think I've ever seen anything like it," Deacon Strong said. "The weather people are still scratching their heads about what caused it. I'll bet your grandfather would've figured it out by now, though."

I felt a lump in my throat. It was not made of ham and cheese sandwich. "What are they saying?" I asked.

"Well, I can't lie. It's not good out there. The snow is about four and a half to five feet now in most places. Six to seven-foot drifts in others. Sounds like the wind and snow are going to get worse before they get better. I'd plan on being inside for a few more days. The plows are having trouble clearing the streets, so even if it stops, you probably won't have school."

"Why are the plows having trouble?" asked Jon.

"There's so much snow in such a short time that it's too heavy for them to move. They're getting stuck."

"Makes me thankful we went grocery shopping on Saturday before the snow got too bad," said Mrs. Strong. "At least we have plenty of food."

I had to think about what she meant by that. "You mean some people don't have food?"

Deacon Strong nodded. "It's possible. There are people who only stock up when they know a big storm is coming, but this storm was a surprise, so they didn't plan for it."

"I never knew snow could cause so much trouble," I said.

"Heavy snow and wind can cause all kinds of problems," said Deacon Strong gently. "People might lose power or heat or even have a roof collapse. It's sad, but it happens sometimes."

My mind raced. Up until now, I didn't think about what using the Snowmallows meant for anyone else. I was worried about me and my stuff

– my test, my grades, my baseball season. But, now, other people might have serious problems because of me thinking only of myself. How had things gotten so complicated? My brow wrinkled. I frowned down at the half-eaten sandwich on my plate. "Wow...a roof collapse," I said softly.

"But, thankfully, we're all fine and have food, lights, and heat," Mrs. Strong said. She reached across the table and put her hand on top of mine as if trying to reassure me. "We have to hope everyone else does, too."

"Amen to that," said Deacon Strong.

"Potato chips." Mrs. Strong popped up from the table. "I forgot the potato chips."

I wasn't in the mood to look at the clock to see how long she sat.

When lunch was over, Deacon Strong said, "Boys, I'll need your help with some shoveling this afternoon. We want David and Emily's parents to have a place to park when they come home."

"Good. Emily and I will bake some cookies while you do that." Mrs. Strong got up to clear the plates from the table.

Deacon Strong glanced out the window. "I think it's snowing too hard to go out right now, though. Let's play a game or watch a movie. Hopefully, by the time we're done, the snow will be falling lighter."

My hope was that it would slow down to a stop, but that seemed like a long shot. I knew we had to get back to the lab, but I wasn't sure what we were going to do once we were there. Maybe the movie and the shoveling would give me an opportunity to think.

CHAPTER 10

Wednesday, March 6 – Mid-Afternoon

It was good that we waited before going out to shovel because the snow was finally falling lighter – not flurries, but better than before. Other than that, it was still miserable outside. The wind was sharp and stung more the longer we stayed outside.

For forty minutes, Jon and I shoveled while Deacon Strong pushed the snow blower. Deacon Strong cleared a one lane path down the driveway from the garage to the front sidewalk. Then he cleared one lane on the sidewalk and one lane down to Molly Fischer's front door, so he could get to her if she needed help. Now he was working on the section of the driveway between the sidewalk and the street. That was the spot I hated shoveling the most because it was usually covered with ice and slush from the snowplow. Was it as bad when the snowplow couldn't get down the street? I was glad I didn't have to find out.

Jon and I cleared the rest of the driveway and now we were working on shoveling the path to our front door. It didn't feel like we were making much progress, though. The snow we shoveled only blew back in our faces in stinging, icy crystals and then landed mostly back where it started. The snowbanks on each side of the path grew until we had to throw the snow onto piles higher than our heads. Melted snow started to soak my baseball cap and ski jacket and my cheeks were red from the cold. The rest of my body was warm from the work and, under my jacket, I was beginning to sweat. Enough was enough.

"Green grass!" I yelled as I tossed a shovelful of snow onto the pile.

"What?" said Jon.

"Green grass! Budding trees!" I heaved another shovelful of snow.

"What are you talking about?"

"I'm trying to make myself feel better by thinking of things I like – things that are warm," I answered.

"Is it working?" Jon asked.

A big gust of wind hit us. Ice prickled my face. "Not really, but I'm positive I like spring way better than this."

Suddenly, an idea hit me that sent a new shiver down my spine – maybe I had the answer. I shoveled as fast as I could. I wanted to get back to the lab.

"Cookies are ready!" called Mrs. Strong.

Deacon Strong, who had finished the end of the driveway, put away the snow blower, picked up a shovel, and helped us finish the path. Then we all headed inside.

We shed our soggy coats and hats in the foyer. Snowball sniffed the soles of the snow-covered shoes we left near the door. Deacon Strong started up the stairs, but before we joined him, I took Jon aside. "I have an idea. Follow my lead."

Upstairs, I took a few cookies off the plate. "Thanks for the cookies, Mrs. Strong. These look great. Do you mind if we take them downstairs and eat them while we watch TV?"

"No problem. Have fun."

As Jon, Emily, Snowball, and I got to the living room downstairs, Jon asked, "Do we really have time to watch TV?"

I shook my head. "No, and we're not going to. I have an idea about the Snowmallows."

"So, you lied to my Mom, Dave?"

"Just a little white Snowmallow lie," I said as I ate a bite of cookie. "I didn't know how else to get back down here."

"Right. Big picture. What's your idea?" asked Jon.

I finished my cookie and licked a little melted chocolate off my finger. "You're probably both going to think I've gone bananas, but you know how the Snowmallows have the things Grandpa likes about winter in them, right?" Emily and Jon nodded. "Well, what if we mix together all the things we like about spring? Maybe it will stop the Snowmallows."

Jon looked skeptical. "Dave, do you really think it's that easy?"

"Probably not, but it's the only idea I have – unless you have another."

Emily shook her head and Jon shrugged his shoulders. "Nope," they both answered, but Emily's answer came out sounding more like "Mope" because her mouth was full of cookies.

"Come on," I said. "Let's search the house for things that remind us of spring, mix them together in the locker, and see what happens. What have we got to lose?"

CHAPTER 11

Wednesday, March 6 – Late Afternoon

J on, Emily, and I split up and searched the house for things that reminded us of spring. It felt like a crazy thing to do in the middle of a snowstorm. Jon covered the living room and bathrooms. Emily, with her furry helper, Snowball, searched the kitchen and all the closets. I checked the bedrooms and rummaged through the basement storage areas.

About two hours later, we met in the lab and spread across the black-topped table the stuff that we found. We had Easter baskets, a package of Bunny's Best sugar coated marshmallow rabbits, photos of our spring flowers and trees from last year, a gardening catalog, some car washing sponges, Dr. Sunshine's All Natural lemonade,

Spring-in-your-Step spring-scented soap, seed packages for different kinds of flowers and vegetables, a baby animal DVD, and, of course, my baseball glove, cleats, and a baseball.

I looked at what we collected. "This is a strange pile of stuff."

"It sure is," said Jon. "And, I have a couple more things upstairs in my room that we can add to it later."

"Like what?" Emily asked.

"I have my baseball glove, some Sneezy and Itchy's Allergy Medication, and a clock that chirps like a different bird every hour."

I raised an eyebrow at him. "Allergy medication and a clock?"

"Not just any clock – it's a *bird* clock. Besides, it's not any stranger than the pile we have now."

I had to agree with him on that.

Emily picked up the package of marshmallow rabbits. "So, what do we do now?"

"Kids! Dinner time!" called Mrs. Strong.

I took the package of marshmallows from Emily and put it back on the table before she had time to snag one. "Sounds like we have dinner."

I put the lemonade in the fridge in the lab and followed Jon, Emily, and Snowball up the stairs.

*

As we sat down to eat and finished our prayer, the phone rang. The caller ID showed that it was Mom's cell. Mrs. Strong jumped up to answer it and put us on speakerphone.

"Mommy!" Emily was so excited she ran toward the phone. Maybe she thought standing next to it would make Mom feel closer.

"Hi, baby. How's it going?"

"Everything's fine, Mom," I said. I hoped I sounded convincing. "How's it going with you?"

"It's going. I miss you guys, though."

"I miss you, too," Emily said. "Are you coming home soon?"

"I was hoping I'd be home tonight, but I don't think that's going to happen."

"Why not?" I could hear the disappointment in Emily's voice.

"Well, the truth is, I'm not sure I can get home. Not many of the roads are clear so, right now, it's safer for me to stay here until the storm ends."

Emily looked like she was trying not to cry. Mrs. Strong stood next to her and gently stroked Emily's hair the way Mom did last night.

"Tess, would you and Mike please keep an eye on the kids until I get home?" Mom asked Mrs. Strong.

"Of course, Audra," said Mrs. Strong. "Don't worry; the kids will be fine with us."

"But what if the storm doesn't stop?" asked Emily.

"Don't be silly, honey. It's going to stop eventually," Mom answered. "I'll be home before you know it."

"We understand, Mom," I said. "Don't worry. We've got this."

Mom sighed. "I know." There was a quiet pause before Mom spoke again. I could tell she was struggling to sound happy. "Well, I've got to run. You two be good and listen to Deacon and Mrs. Strong. I love you and I'll see you *soon*." She emphasized the word "soon".

"We love you, too." Again, Emily and I said it at the same time.

None of us kids ate much for dinner, although Snowball's appetite seemed healthy. Emily slipped some pieces of chicken to him under the table. I managed to eat my chicken, but I had so many questions and worries inside me that my mind and stomach were both already churning. I pushed the rest of my rice and beans around on my plate with my fork as I thought. How many people didn't have food and power because of the storm? How long would Emily and I be separated from the rest of our family? Would our idea for stopping the storm work? All I knew was that I had to get back to the lab and try to make things right.

Mrs. Strong looked worried when she saw our half-full plates. "Gee, I thought my cooking was better than that. Maybe next time I'll just serve ice cream. At least that might get you guys to smile."

Deacon Strong was the only one who laughed, but his smile faded quickly. Mrs. Strong got up and fixed a plate of cookies for dessert.

"Look, I know you're worried about your parents," said Deacon Strong. "But they'll be home before you know it."

Emily, Jon, and I stayed quiet.

Mrs. Strong put the cookies on the table. Deacon Strong was the only one to reach for them.

"No cookies, either?"

Mrs. Strong picked up the plate and walked around the table to each of us a few times. On each round, Deacon Strong was the only one to take a cookie. Finally, he gently removed the plate from his wife's hands and set it on the table to stop the cookie train. Mrs. Strong got the message and sat down.

"You know, guys," Deacon Strong said, "it'll be bedtime soon. So, why don't we head downstairs and get your pajamas and sleeping bags and bring them up here."

"What a great idea," said Mrs. Strong. "The boys can take showers – which I'm sure they need after shoveling – and then we can all watch a little TV and play with Snowball before we go to sleep. I'm sure things will be better if we relax and get a good night's sleep."

It was the opening I needed. "I think so, too, but would it be all right if Emily and I slept downstairs in our own beds?" I asked. "I think we'll be more comfortable."

Jon spoke up. "Can I sleep downstairs, too, Mom? Dave has twin beds in his room."

"I don't know." Mrs. Strong looked over at Deacon Strong. "Mike, do you think it's a good idea?"

"I don't see any harm in it," Deacon Strong replied. "You said earlier yourself there wasn't much they could do during this storm."

Jon gave his Mom a pleading look. "Besides, Mom, you're right upstairs if we need anything."

Mrs. Strong sighed heavily. "I guess it's fine for tonight."

Jon kissed his Mom's cheek. "Thanks, Mom."

"Not so fast," said Mrs. Strong. "I want both of you boys to take showers and I want all of you in bed before nine."

"I'll come down to check on you and to say prayers at eight thirty," said Deacon Strong. "That way we're sure you're following instructions."

While Jon hurried to take his shower and gather his things, Emily and I helped put away the leftovers and clear our plates from the table. Deacon Strong showed his wife his empty plate as he set it in the sink. "See, honey, I liked your cooking."

Mrs. Strong smiled and gently tossed him a blue, gingham dishtowel. Deacon Strong was drying the last of the dishes as Jon came back into the kitchen. He was wearing sweats and had a full backpack over his shoulder.

"What's with the backpack?" asked the Deacon. "Are you planning to move in down there?"

Jon laughed and shrugged. "Never know what you'll need," he said. I knew he wasn't going to say anything else that might make him have to lie to his parents.

I thanked Jon's parents for the food and wished them a good night's sleep. Emily, Jon, Snowball, and I headed for the door leading down to our part of the house. When it closed behind Jon's backpack without any more questions from his parents, I felt like we'd successfully jumped a big hurdle.

CHAPTER 12

Wednesday, March 6 – Bedtime

When we got downstairs, Jon was all business. "So, what's your plan, Dave?"

"For starters, I think Emily and I should get ready for bed."

"What?" Jon asked.

"Jon, your Dad's going to check on us in about an hour and a half to make sure we're in bed. So, if we want to stay down here to work on our problem, we'd better be ready for bed when he comes."

"But what about Mom and Dad? We need to fix the Snowmallows so they can come home." Emily didn't even try to hold back her tears this time.

I handed her a pink tissue from the box on the end table and put my arm around her. "I want them to come home, too, Em. So, while you and I get ready for bed, Jon's going to go down to the lab. He'll get Grandpa's notes so we can look at them again, and he'll make a list of the spring things we found. Then when Deacon Strong leaves, we'll work on stopping the snow."

Emily took a deep breath in through her nose and let it out through her mouth, just like Mom taught her to do when she needed to calm down. This time, the breath in sounded more like the broken, snuffled sort of breath you have when you're sobbing, but it still did the trick. She nodded, wiped her eyes on the pink tissue, and blew her nose. "I'll go put on my pjs."

Emily and I were done getting ready for bed by the time Jon came back from the lab. We looked at Grandpa's notes until just before 8:30 and, when Deacon Strong came downstairs, we made sure we were all in our sleeping places in my room – Emily and I were in each of the twin beds and Jon was on the floor between us in my sleeping bag. Snowball was on Emily's lap. He pawed at the covers while she petted him.

"Nice job, you guys," said Deacon Strong. There was a touch of surprise in his voice. "You did exactly what we asked."

"You of little faith." Jon shook his head at his father.

Deacon Strong laughed. "Speaking of faith, who's ready for prayers?"

"David and Emily don't usually pray at bedtime," said Jon.

I thought it was nice of him to add the words "at bedtime" since he knew we didn't usually pray anytime.

Deacon Strong sat down on the end of Emily's bed. "No worries, Jon. You and I will pray." Jon's Dad looked at me. "Are you guys comfortable if we pray here? Would you like us to go back upstairs?"

I looked over at Emily and she shrugged her shoulders.

"You can stay here," I said. Besides, I didn't want to take a chance that Jon might get stuck upstairs.

Deacon Strong nodded. "Thank you," he said, "feel free to jump in if the spirit moves."

"Moves where?" asked Emily.

Deacon Strong smiled at her but didn't answer the question. He and Jon bowed their heads. Then the Deacon began. "Lord, thank you for bringing us safely to the end of another day. It's been a long day for many, but we know you've been with all of us. Thank you, too, for the many blessings you've given. In a special way, I want to thank you that Molly Fischer has what she needs to get through the storm. I was worried about her, but you took care of things. Please continue to watch over all impacted by this weather and help us with our needs. Forgive our failings and grant us a restful night's sleep." Deacon Strong paused. "Jon, would you like to add anything?"

"Please keep Dave and Emily's family safe while they're away. And help us so the storm stops soon so they can come home."

"Amen to that," said Deacon Strong. "In your mercy, Lord, please hear our prayers. We trust in you. Amen."

Emily watched Deacon Strong and Jon closely as they prayed. When they finished, she asked Deacon Strong, "Why do you pray?"

"Prayer is how I talk with God," said Deacon Strong.

"I get that part. But why? Isn't he supposed to already know everything?"

Deacon Strong smiled. "Yes, he does. And I think that's the best reason to talk with him – because he knows everything, and I don't."

Emily nodded. "My Grandpa is really smart, too, so I talk to him about lots of things."

"That's a great analogy, Emily," said Deacon Strong. "God and I talk about lots of things, too. I feel like he is a part of my family, just like your Grandpa is part of yours. Sometimes I tell him about my day. Other times I ask for his help. I thank him for things. Then, I try to listen to him speak to my heart."

"And does your heart hear him?" Emily asked.

"Sometimes I feel like I hear him clearly, but not always. When I feel peaceful about something, that's usually his voice."

Emily sat quietly for a moment, but I could tell by the look on her face that she still wanted to know something.

"Deacon Strong, when you ask for help, does God help you?" asked Emily.

"Well, that depends. Sometimes God's answer is no. Other times he answers, and things work out just as I hope. Then there are times when he answers yes, but in a way I don't expect."

"What does that mean?" asked Emily.

Deacon Strong rubbed his chin as he thought. "Well, let me give you an example. A few weeks ago, I couldn't find my reading glasses."

Jon gave a little snort as he stifled a laugh. Emily frowned at him. "Sorry," said Jon. "It's just that this story always makes me laugh."

Deacon Strong chuckled. "Would you like to tell the story, son?"

Jon shook his head. "No. It's way funnier when you tell it."

"So, I guess I'm acting it out, too?"

"Of course," said Jon.

Deacon Strong turned back to Emily. "So, anyway, one day I couldn't find my reading glasses. I thought I put them down on the coffee table when I finished the morning paper," he pretended to scan an imaginary coffee table, "but they weren't there."

The slight grin on his face as he made the pretend movements made Emily smile and straighten up in bed.

Deacon Strong stood up and scanned the top of my bookcase. "I looked high."

He squatted down and looked under Emily's bed. "I even searched low."

Emily giggled, especially when Snowball lifted his head to see what Deacon Strong was doing.

Deacon Strong stood up again and scratched Snowball behind the ears. "I searched for a little while, but I was running late for an appointment. So, I prayed that God would help me find them."

He folded his hands and closed his eyes like he was praying. Then he opened his eyes wide and lifted his pointer finger in the air like when you say, "ah ha!". "Almost immediately, I got the idea to re-trace my steps from that morning. I went back to where I was reading on the sofa," Deacon Strong sat down on the end of Emily's bed again.

"CRUNCH!" he said, "I sat right on them and cracked them in half."

Jon and I laughed out loud.

"Oh no! What did you do then?" asked Emily.

"I was upset at first, but the truth is that I really needed a new pair of glasses. I kept putting off getting an eye exam because I didn't think I had the time. So, God not only helped me find my glasses, but he also prompted me to get a new pair that worked better for me. Did God give me what I asked for? Yes. Was it in the way I wanted him to do it? Not at all. Was it better in the end? Absolutely."

"But what did you do about your appointment that day? How did you see?" asked Emily.

"I got a big ol' piece of blue electrical tape and taped the glasses down the middle of the nosepiece. They looked awful and I felt cross-eyed all morning. I was so embarrassed that I went to the eye doctor that afternoon."

Emily laughed. "So, things turned out good because God gave you what you needed, even if it wasn't how you wanted?"

"That's right."

I knew the point he was trying to make, but I wondered if he was right. "How do you know it wasn't just coincidence?" I asked.

Deacon Strong nodded. "Good question. Some might call it coincidence, but I call it a God moment. Faith tells me it's an answer to my prayer."

That made me think. What was it like to have that kind of trust in someone you couldn't see?

I didn't know what else to say, but Emily still seemed to be full of questions. "What about if you need help because you did something wrong and you want to fix it? Does he help you then?"

"That's probably when we need his help the most, so I think he's very happy when we turn to him then," answered Deacon Strong.

"May I talk to him?" asked Emily.

"Sure, Emily."

"Do I have to talk to him out loud?"

"No, you can speak to him in your heart. He'll hear you."

Emily closed her eyes and bowed her head like she saw Jon and Deacon Strong do. I could only imagine what she must be saying to God. It was probably something like, "Hi God. My brother's the one that used the Snowmallows and messed up all your nice weather. So, please help him fix it because he has no idea what he's doing, and I need my parents to come home."

Unfortunately, I couldn't argue much if that was what she was saying because it was true. *God,* I thought, *I don't know if you're there or not, but, if you are, would you please point me in the right direction down here? Please help me fix what's wrong.*

When Emily looked like she'd finished her prayer, Deacon Strong asked, "All set, Emily?"

"Yes, thank you."

Deacon Strong stood up. "So, I guess you're sleeping in here instead of in your room?"

"Yes," she said.

Deacon Strong looked quizzically over at Jon. "We're good, Dad," said Jon. "Emily didn't want to be alone and I'm comfy down here."

Deacon Strong raised a concerned eyebrow. "Emily, are you sure there isn't anything bothering you that you want to talk about?"

"No, thank you. I'm good. I talked to God." She settled into bed. Snowball curled up in the crook of her arm.

Deacon Strong shrugged. "Going straight to the top man. How can I argue with that?" He gave Snowball another scratch on the head. Snowball gave him a contented blink. "Good night. Sleep tight. And, don't worry, the snow should stop soon."

"Night, Dad," said Jon.

Deacon Strong turned off the light and closed the door. I heard him climb the stairs. But, instead of a quiet night where we could sleep tight, the wind outside whistled and whipped as the storm continued to rage.

CHAPTER 13

Wednesday, March 6 – During the Night

When it sounded like the coast was clear, I pulled my camping lantern from under my bed and turned it on.

"You keep a camping lantern under your bed?" asked Jon.

"I've been using it to stay up late and study. I can't leave the overhead light on when Mom and Dad think I'm sleeping, can I?"

"Imagine what you could do if you used your powers for good," said Jon wistfully as he got off the floor and sat on the edge of my bed. "Right, Emily?"

Except for some contented purring coming from Snowball, there was no answer from the other bed. I wasn't sure if it was the prayers or the warm cat cuddled up next to her that did the trick, but Emily was fast asleep. Jon didn't look too far behind her, but he fought it. We looked at Grandpa's notes and the list of spring items for about another two hours. We came up with some possible ideas for inverting the temperature and drying the water out of the clouds, but we had a long way to go.

As we worked, I wondered what would've made Grandpa invent the Snowmallows in the first place, especially if he never planned to use them outside. I guess it was just another thing to add to the "weird stuff I don't understand about my Grandpa" list. I'm not sure why, but the whole situation made me a little angry at him. I had no time to focus on that, though. Right now, I had to deal with cleaning up my own mess.

I threw another idea in Jon's direction, but his chin was sinking toward his chest as he dozed off. I gently shook his shoulder. He jumped.

"Sorry, Dave, I'm wiped out. I think we should sleep for a couple of hours and try again later. I just can't think anymore."

"I agree. Go to sleep. I want to watch the news for a few minutes to see what they're saying now."

Jon dropped into the sleeping bag while I took the camping lantern to the living room and turned on the TV. I kept the volume low so no one else would hear it. The cancellations were scrolling at the bottom of the screen showing that we didn't have school again tomorrow.

"How's it going, Brian?" asked Carla the Anchorwoman. She was wearing a golf shirt with the channel logo on it instead of the dress she had on that morning. She also had glasses on now and her eyelids looked dark and heavy. What happened to Larry? Was he somewhere taking a nap, like Jon?

"I don't know, Carla," said Brian. He nervously brushed his fingers through his tousled hair. His tie was crooked and loose, and a corner of his dress shirt was untucked. "It looks like we have a slight lull in the action for now, but who knows when that will change again."

"Maybe it means we're coming to the end of this storm," suggested Carla.

"That would be nice, but I have no data to confirm that. And, unfortunately, when the snow finally does stop, it's still going to cause problems."

"Why is that?"

I was glad Carla asked that question since I was wondering the same thing.

"Well, Carla, during March, when the days are getting longer, this volume of snow will melt faster than during the dead of winter. However, it could still take a while. If it melts quickly, there could be flooding in low lying areas. If it takes longer, it could result in roof collapses by melting and refreezing. I'm all out of ideas about where we go from here."

"I think the plow drivers are too," said Carla. "They've started using pay loaders and dump trucks to move the snow to open fields and parks to try to get it out of the way. It's become too heavy for the equipment they normally use."

I didn't want to watch the footage of the pay loaders, so I went to the window and looked out for the first time since shoveling that afternoon. Brian on TV was right. The snow was coming down very lightly. Everything was still. It was amazing how quiet it got when there were no cars driving down the street or people talking outside. And when the snow fell in front of the streetlights, it glistened in icy sparkles. When it was like this, I could almost understand what Grandpa might like about winter.

On the flip side, the snow piles were huge. They had to be at least six feet in places that weren't shoveled. I knew then that even if we could stop the snow and warm things up again, Brian the Meteorologist was probably right. There was no way to tell how long it would take to clear the roads or for the snow piles to melt. Baseball season at Fairlane Park would be impossible. The pay loaders would be dumping the plowed snow into piles on those fields to get it off the roads and those piles would take forever to melt. But baseball wasn't the important thing right now. Wow! That thought stopped me in my tracks. Only a few days ago, baseball was my biggest worry, but not anymore. Now I was worried about my neighbors, my friends, and, especially, my family.

I glanced at the TV. Brian and Carla were back on the screen.

"Well, there are weather patterns that could help the plow guys by clearing and drying up the snow quickly," said Brian. "And since they're almost as unlikely as this snowstorm, it's anybody's guess right now as to if we'll see those too."

"Well, that's Brian the Meteorologist's ray of sunshine for today," said Carla.

Wait...was that true? Could we find a way to melt the snow and dry the ground quickly? I turned off the TV and went to find as many weather books as I could. It looked like I had more studying to do.

CHAPTER 14

Thursday, March 7 – Before Dawn

One minute I was reading a book and the next minute...*I could see my parents standing in front of a backstop on a ball field at Fairlane Park. The grass was thick and green. Violets and clover grew all around their feet. Pink and white blossoms covered the dogwood trees. Then I saw Emily running toward them with Snowball standing on her head. Wait...why was Snowball standing on her head? Suddenly, a snowplow pushed a dirt covered, icy pile of snow between her and our parents. Emily tried to climb over it, but then a payloader dumped the snow from its bucket on top of her, burying her up to her waist. I ran to help. Frantically, I dug with both arms at the side of the pile to get her out, but I wasn't fast enough. Another bucket load of snow dumped on Emily until the tip of Snowball's tail was buried. No!*

I sat bolt upright in my bed. My arms were still digging Emily out of the snow. I was panting and my heart was pounding. The books I was reading just before I dozed off slid over the side of the bed. They thudded in a haphazard heap on top of Jon. Some were open. Some were closed. Jon mumbled an "Ow". The whole mess was enough to startle Snowball. He flew off Emily's bed and landed on top of the pile of books that hit Jon. Snowball tried to run, but he couldn't get any traction. His front feet flipped the slippery pages of the open books like a paper treadmill. Finally, Snowball dug his back claws hard through my sleeping bag and into a little bit of Jon's arms. Then the cat leapt across the books onto Jon's legs, and with another leap, was out the door.

"Ouch!" said Jon. He was still groggy when I bent down and started to take the books off him. "There are kinder ways to wake a person up. What time is it?"

"Sorry, Jon. It's four in the morning. I fell asleep trying to find something in these books, but I couldn't..." I paused as I noticed a page in an open book. Wait...what was this? I couldn't believe it. It was the answer I was searching for last night. Snowball found it when his feet shuffled the open pages. I wondered if this was because of my prayer. I wasn't sure, but I whispered a quick "Thank You" just to be safe. I quickly helped Jon out from under the rest of the book pile.

"Jon, I think I know what we need to do." I shook Emily. "Emily, wake up and get dressed. We're heading to the lab."

* * *

It took a few minutes to get Jon and Emily moving, but I was too excited to let them dawdle. The fact that the storm got worse overnight also added to my need for speed. It almost felt like the blustering wind outside was blowing us down to the lab. Snowball followed closely behind Emily and peered around her feet whenever she stopped. I didn't know if the snow was making him nervous or if he was haunted by the early morning book avalanche.

When we got to the lab, I got right to the point. "What we need to do is create a chinook."

"What's that?" asked Emily. She yawned and rubbed her eyes.

"It's a warm, dry wind to change the winter weather to spring," I said. "I read about it in a book. I hope we have what we need."

Jon sat on one of the stools with an alcohol pad nursing one of the deeper cat scratches on his arm. The bathroom was one of the few stops I allowed before we came down to the lab, so he'd grabbed what he needed to nurse his cuts. "Glad there was a sleeping bag between me and those claws, Snowball."

Snowball peeked out from behind Emily when Jon said his name.

"Please don't be mad at Snowball," said Emily. "He was just scared. I'm sure he's sorry."

"It's not really his fault, Emily." Jon put a bandage over the scratch. "I can't blame Snowball for Dave's nightmare."

I sighed. I knew Jon wasn't talking about the bad dream that woke me this morning.

"So, where do we start?" Jon asked.

I gave Jon a sheepish look. "I think we need to start by mixing more Snowmallows."

"You're kidding, right? Did you forget what's outside?" asked Jon.

I took a step back from Jon. "You get kind of scary and sarcastic when you're tired."

"And wounded," he said, pointing to his punctured arm. "Don't forget wounded."

"Look," I said, "I'm sorry about *all* of it. Of course, I remember what's happening out there, but I think this is the right move." I went to the shelf and got a mug. "Besides, we're not going to use them outside. This time we're going to mix them in the weather locker. Then, one by one, we'll add the springtime items that we think can stop the Snowmallows and see if they work."

"That actually sounds like a good plan. Let's get started," said Emily.

Jon's mouth dropped open. "You're agreeing to use more Snowmallows? Who are you and what have you done with Emily Griffin?"

Emily shrugged and yawned. "David's idea sounds like what Grandpa would do. Grandpa does tests like that in the weather locker all the time."

"Come on, Jon," I said. "It's the only way to test our formula without messing up the outside weather even more. We have to try."

Jon ran his fingers through his hair and huffed. "If the cat had a vote, he'd side with Emily, so it looks like I'm outnumbered."

Snowball was calmer since being forgiven, so he gave Jon a disinterested yawn and curled into a ball in the palm of my baseball glove. That probably meant the cat wasn't voting, but I wasn't going to point out that Jon was still outnumbered.

I started climbing the stairs to the kitchen. "I'll go mix some cocoa."

"Why don't we just use instant? It'll be faster," said Jon.

I shook my head. "No. I think we need to do things the way Grandpa would. I read something last night about a theory called the Butterfly Effect. It says that even small differences in how we do something from one time to the next can completely change the outcome."

Jon lifted his eyebrows at me. "Look who's paying attention to science now."

I laughed. It was ironic. "Besides, we'd have to get instant from your kitchen. Do you want to explain to your parents why we need instant cocoa at 4 a.m.?"

"Point taken," Jon said.

*   *   *

I slid a mug of hot cocoa through the door at the bottom of the weather locker. Then I dropped two Snowmallows into the liquid so quickly some cocoa splashed over the side. I almost caught my fingers in the door as I slammed it. I didn't want any of that stuff to escape. The mixture foamed and crashed like before and flurries began to fall from a cloud inside the locker.

I looked at Jon's and my notes from last night, especially the list of springtime favorites we collected. "I think we should start with lemonade.

We said last night that ice cold lemonade would be good to counteract hot cocoa. Right?"

"Let's try it," answered Jon.

I poured lemonade into another mug. I slid the mug through as small an opening in the locker door as I could manage before quickly closing it again. A few snowflakes landed in the mug. The lemonade began to bubble. Some of it evaporated. Right away we heard a pinging sound inside the locker. It sounded like Fruity O's hitting the bottom of an empty cereal bowl.

"It's sleeting," Jon said.

I closed my eyes and thought out loud. "That means that the lemonade made some of the higher air colder when it evaporated. So, it isn't cold enough to snow, but it isn't warm enough to just rain, either."

"So, it still needs to be warmer?" asked Emily.

I nodded.

Emily handed me a seed package. "Then let's add some chili pepper seeds. You know Dad always sweats when he eats the peppers from the garden."

I tried Emily's suggestion and dropped a few of the seeds into the lemonade. The pinging sound changed to a splashing sound.

"It looks like it's working," I said. "The sleet is turning to rain. Good suggestion, Em."

Emily thrust her fists into the air. "Yes! One step closer to Mom and Dad coming home."

"Wait, something's not right." I took a closer look through the locker glass. "The mug is coated in ice. It looks like it's frozen to the bottom of the locker."

Emily's arms dropped back to her sides like deflated balloons. "What happened?"

"Freezing rain," said Jon. "The ground is still too cold, so the rain freezes when it hits."

I stared at the icy floor of the locker. "Maybe we can't reverse the Snowmallows. None of the other things we brought are going to make the ground warmer. Now what do we do?"

CHAPTER 15

Thursday, March 7 – Dawn

I leaned my elbow on the black-topped table and rested my head in my hand. As we thought about what to do next, Emily sat on the other stool near my baseball glove and petted Snowball's long fur.

Almost immediately, John's eyes closed, and his nose wrinkled. "Achoo! Emily, please stop petting that cat. All his fur is flying off him and going up my nose again."

"Sorry, but I told you – petting Snowball helps me think."

I stood up straight. "Hey, maybe Snowball can help."

"See, you help David think, too," Emily whispered to the purring kitty.

Jon rubbed his eyes. "Maybe I'm missing something, but how can a cat named *Snowball* help us melt ice?"

"When he sits on my lap, he's warmer than a blanket," I said. "Maybe if we put some of his fur in the formula, it can make the ground warm, too."

"And he was born last spring," Emily added.

Neither one of us hesitated. Emily and I rubbed our hands across Snowball's back as Jon covered his face with his hands. Snowball purred loudly from all the attention. When we had a good size handful, I put the fur on top of the frozen lemonade mug. The ice melted from around the mug and puddles began running down the drain in the bottom of the locker.

"It worked!" said Emily.

The only problem was that rubbing the cat built up a small static charge in the fur and caused a few stray bolts of lightning to light up the locker.

Snowball moved from the baseball glove to the black-topped table to give himself a bath. He seemed to be saying, "Yes, it worked. Cats rule and people's hands are grimy."

I checked the notes again. "We're making progress. Now we have to get the dirt out of the air so no more raindrops will form."

Jon held up the bar of Spring-in-Your-Step spring scented soap. "Let's try this."

"Sounds like a plan." I took the spoon I used to mix the cocoa and scraped off a few curly shards of soap. I added the soap shavings to the lemonade along with a corner of the car wash sponge. I thought the sponge might soak up the water that was still falling from the clouds. It helped, but it wasn't quite enough to stop the rain completely.

"Look," said Jon. "It's virga."

"Who's that?" Emily asked.

I chuckled. "It's not a who, it's a what. Virga is when rain falls from the clouds but evaporates before it hits the ground." Adding a little more sponge did the trick. It stopped the rain and dried the ground.

"Now, we just need wind to fan the clouds back to the ocean," said Jon.

At that moment, I felt completely confident that I had the right answer. "I know the perfect spring wind for fanning – Griffin's Greatest Fastball!"

"Strikes out the batter every time," Jon said.

I tossed Jon his glove and pointed to one end of the basement. "Jon, stand over there."

Then I asked Emily to get an empty mason jar off one of the shelves. While she did that, I plucked a couple of stray cat hairs off my glove, grabbed it and the ball, and headed to the opposite side of the basement.

"Em," I said, "you kneel on the floor between us and, when I throw the fastball to Jon, you catch the wind from it in the jar. Got it?"

Emily knelt on the floor midway between us. "Don't hit me."

After a few tries, Emily caught the wind in the jar and covered it with the lid. I slid the jar into the locker. As fast as I could, I removed the lid, tipped the jar over the lemonade mug to pour out the fastball, pulled the jar back out, and closed the locker door.

"How will we know if it does anything?" asked Jon. "We can't see air."

I looked at the cloud sitting at the top of the locker. "I think the cloud is trying to move. See it?"

Emily nodded. "I see it. It's starting to circle the top of the locker."

She was right. The cloud was circling because, inside the locker, it had nowhere to go. It spun and spun, faster and faster until it formed the funnel of a small tornado. The locker began to groan and shake. I was afraid the bolts holding the locker to the floor might come loose at any minute. Snowball ran toward the door of the lab.

"Oh no!" yelled Jon.

"Quick, Em, head for the door!" I grabbed her hand. "I think it's gonna blow!"

CHAPTER 16

Thursday, March 7 – Early Morning

As I was about to open the lab door, I heard something. "Coo. Coo. Coo-hoo-oo. Coo-hoo-oo. Coo. Coo." Jon's bird clock signaled six with the sound of a mourning dove. The groaning and shaking stopped. I glanced back at the locker. The sound of the doves made the tornado vanish as quickly as it started. Inside the locker, the weather was clear.

"Guess that's our hopeful sound of the season." I leaned against the door and blew out a heavy breath of relief.

Emily picked up Snowball and kissed his head. Jon came over to me and we exchanged a high five, a low five, and a quick jog in place for a count of five.

"What was that?" Emily asked.

I smiled at her. "Our victory handshake."

Emily lifted an eyebrow. "I don't think we won yet, so don't jinx us."

"But," said Jon, "I think since we just survived a tornado, it fits. Besides, it's really fun."

"Sure." Emily rolled her eyes and took a seat on one of the stools near the table. She started picking through the pile of spring items.

I thought she was trying to tell us to get back to work, so I focused on what we still had to do. "Now," I said, "we need to combine the spring things into one mix, like Grandpa did with the Snowmallows, so they add evenly to the lemonade. That should not only stop the snow, but it should also melt what's already fallen. So, what do you think? How do we hold it all together?"

"Wha?" said Emily in a sticky, full mouthed voice. Apparently, I was wrong about her wanting to get back to work.

"Are you eating our spring stuff?" Jon pointed to a headless Bunny's Best marshmallow rabbit in Emily's hand.

Emily swallowed. "I was hungry. We didn't have any breakfast. Do you want one?"

I nodded. "Yes, Emily. I do want one."

"Actually, I was asking Jon. Marshmallows make you sick, David."

"Yes, they do. I think they're completely disgusting," I said. "But I'm not going to eat it. I'm going to follow Grandpa's lead and use it to hold together our formula for...by the way, what should we call this stuff?"

"Chinook-ade" was Jon's suggestion. "Meltmallows" was Emily's.

Then I thought of the perfect name. "Let's call it...Lemonthaw," I said.

"I like that name," said Emily.

"Lemonthaw it is," Jon agreed.

I took two marshmallow rabbits and sliced them in half long ways. I set the halves next to each other like slices of bread for my lunch. Then I turned each one into a small sandwich full of chili pepper seeds, cat fur, Spring-In-Your-Step soap shavings, pieces of car wash sponge, and Griffin's Greatest fastball wind. When I put the halves back together, it surprised me that marshmallows could be even more repulsive to me than before.

Jon made a sick-looking face. "Well, they look just as stomach-churning as the Snowmallows. Hopefully that means they'll work."

Jon and I took the Lemonthaw rabbits, two mugs, and the carton of lemonade and carried them out to the porch. Emily carried Snowball. We all stood for a moment watching the steadily falling snow.

"Are you sure about this, Dave?" asked Jon.

I shrugged. "Your guess is as good as mine, Jon, but I really wish you'd stop asking me that question."

"I'm scared," said Emily.

I put my hand on her shoulder. "Me, too, but it worked in the lab. There's no reason it shouldn't work here, right?"

"I agree," said Jon, "but maybe we should leave the front door open just in case we need to run for cover."

That was a good suggestion. "Right." I opened the front door and left it that way. Then I set two mugs of lemonade on a large snow drift at the top of the porch stairs. "Well, here goes nothin'."

"And I wish you'd stop saying that," said Jon.

I cautiously dropped the Lemonthaw rabbits into the mugs and stood back. As some of the snowflakes fell into the mugs, the lemonade fizzed a little. Some of the snow started changing over to rain, but nothing was happening as fast as it did in the lab.

I scratched my head. "Did we forget something?"

Just then, the cuckoo clock in the foyer sounded seven cuckoos through the open door. The Lemonthaw mixture began to bubble yellow foam that frothed over the sides of the mugs. Even though that seemed more like what should happen, I wasn't sure if it made me feel better or not.

Sparks of electricity popped from the mugs as they shattered. "Look, more lightning," said Emily.

Snowball, who was calm up until then, jumped from Emily's arms and started running in circles chasing his tail. Jon hopped out of his way.

Soon, a soft wind encircled us with the scent of spring air, and, in minutes, the snow stopped falling. The temperature climbed to 70 degrees and the snow on the ground evaporated making a thick fog that lifted quickly. I felt my shoulders drop. As I saw what was happening around me, I finally relaxed.

"It's just what we hoped would happen. It's stopping as fast as it started," I said.

In the western sky, the wall of storm clouds began to sail over our heads toward the ocean. Then the sun peeked through some cracks in the clouds behind us.

"Snowball, look at the pretty rainbow," said Emily. Snowball wasn't listening, though. He was running frantically down the porch steps and around the corner of the house.

"What's the matter with him?" asked Jon.

Emily looked worried. "I don't know. I've never seen him like this."

"Maybe we should catch him before he hurts himself," I said.

Jon and Emily ran after Snowball while I waited by the porch stairs to grab the cat as he went by. I missed Snowball the first two times he circled the house. Then, as Snowball started his third loop, I heard the phone ringing inside. I ran to answer it.

"Hello?"

"Hi, Honey."

"Hi, Mom. How's it going?" I tried to catch my breath.

"Everything all right? You sound winded."

"Just playing with Snowball. He's full of energy this morning."

"That's good. I'm glad there's nothing wrong," said Mom. "Anyway, we were just listening to Brian the Meteorologist. Looks like the storm's over. Some other crazy weather pattern came through and cleared the snow. Dad and I will be home as soon as the replacement staff members arrive."

That made me smile wider than I had in a while. "That's great! Maybe we can all go for a walk later."

"That sounds nice, but wouldn't you rather go to Fairlane Park and play baseball?"

Normally that would have been my number one activity, but today I felt differently about it. "I've got all spring to do that," I answered.

"See you soon," said Mom. "I love you."

"I love you, too."

I went back outside to help with Emily's cat. A little while later, the phone rang again.

"Hello?"

"David is that you? It's Grandpa. I have some questions about the weather up there."

CHAPTER 17

Thursday, March 7 – Morning

Normally, I would've passed the phone to Emily rather than talk to Grandpa myself, but I had a bad feeling I should handle this one.

"Hi, Grandpa. Where are you?"

"I'm on a plane from Miami to New York. I'm trying to come home, but I understand there's been some unusual weather and I might have trouble getting back. What's going on up there?"

"We had a few feet of snow yesterday, but it's gone now. You shouldn't have any problems getting home."

"Really?" Grandpa sounded surprised. "You had a few feet of snow *yesterday* and it's gone?"

I was afraid to answer. "Yes...?" I said in a guilty sounding voice.

"Do you mean that the snow stopped? Or do you mean that it isn't on the ground anymore?"

"Um...both?" I sensed I might be in trouble in a moment or two.

"David, do you know if anyone's been in my lab while I've been gone?"

A cold shiver prickled down my arms. I gave the safest answer I could to his question. "What makes you think someone's been in your lab?"

"Well, two things. One is that several feet of snow from yesterday disappeared already and the only explanation I have for that is in my lab. And the other is that my plane is flying upside down right now. I'm not sure if that's because of what's in my lab, but it's certainly possible."

I shook my head in disbelief. "Grandpa, did you say your plane is flying upside down?"

"Well, it was a moment ago, but now it seems to be turning in a slow corkscrew." Grandpa made a sick sounding groan.

"Grandpa, you're not going to get sick, are you?"

"Not sure. Never liked roller coasters." I could tell by the shortened sentences that he was trying to keep his breakfast down. "Please answer."

I didn't really want to, but, under the circumstances, I decided it would be better to come clean before I caused a whole plane full of people to throw up. I gave Grandpa a quick summary of how I used the Snowmallows and of how Jon, Emily, and I created the reversal formula in the weather locker. I told him we'd used the Lemonthaw outside almost an hour ago and that the weather was now clear. "So, that means that everything's fine now, right?"

"Not really. My plane's flitting around like a butterfly."

Like a butterfly? The word struck me.

"Grandpa, I think I know what's going on. We'll fix it. Just hang in there."

"Ohhhhh...I'm upside down again. Hanging's the only choice."

I set the phone receiver on the side table and ran down to the lab two steps at a time to get Jon's bird clock. I rushed back upstairs and outside to where Jon and Emily had cornered Snowball next to the porch steps. The cat's front paws were wrapped around a garden gnome's pointed blue hat, while his back paws were kicking its painted red coat. Jon sneezed repeatedly. As I took the batteries out of Jon's clock, I told them what was happening to Grandpa.

"Do you remember the Butterfly Effect – that theory I told you about?"

"Yeah," said Jon. "It's that theory that says that only slight differences in how something is done can change the outcome."

I nodded. "I think that's the problem with Grandpa's plane. When we used the Lemonthaw in the locker, it was the mourning dove cooing six times on your clock that made it work. But, when we came outside, it worked when the cuckoo clock in the foyer hit seven. I think that difference is why Grandpa's plane is acting weird."

Jon pulled a tissue out of his pocket to blow his nose. "A cuckoo would seem like a good explanation for what's happening to him."

"And to Snowball." Emily pointed to the cat who was biting the tip of the garden gnome's hat. "So how do we fix it?"

I looked at the face of Jon's clock. "What's the bird for seven o'clock?"

Jon didn't even need to look at it. "It's a bald eagle."

"That sounds like a great bird for counteracting a cuckoo," I said. I went inside, turned the clock's hands back around the dial to seven o'clock, replaced the batteries, and let the clock chime seven eagle screeches from inside the house.

Emily called to me from outside. "Snowball just dropped the garden gnome. He's calm again."

A moment later, the winds started to pick up and swirl like they did in the locker just before the tornado.

"Oh, no!" Emily said as she grabbed Snowball.

Jon pulled Emily into the foyer. "Hurry, Dave!"

I took the clock's batteries out again, turned it back to six, and ran out to the porch. As the wind battered my face with the dry dirt from the yard,

I replaced the batteries. The mourning dove began to coo. At the sound of the sixth coo, the wind died off.

"Do you think it worked?" asked Jon.

"There's only one way to find out." I ran back into the house and picked up the phone receiver. "Grandpa, are you there?"

"Yes, I'm here," he said calmly. "I just called to let your parents know that I'd be landing in about an hour, so they can pick me up at Terminal 2."

"Is your plane flying right side up now?"

"Of course. What makes you think it wouldn't be?"

CHAPTER 18

Thursday, March 7 – Before School

What was going on?

"Grandpa, didn't you just tell me your plane was flying upside down?" I asked.

"No...Guess it must be a bad connection." Grandpa talked louder. "I just told you to ask your parents to pick me up at Terminal 2 in an hour. See you soon."

Grandpa hung up before I could tell him that Mom and Dad weren't home.

I hung up the receiver. "That was strange."

"So, what's going on?" asked Jon. "Is the plane flying right side up again?"

"I'm not sure."

Jon looked confused. "It was a yes or no question. What do you mean you're not sure?"

"You know, I knew Grandpa was weird, but this was one of the strangest conversations ever. When I just talked to him, it sounded like nothing was wrong with the plane in the first place. I think Grandpa's losing it!"

"What are you talking about?" asked Emily.

"He asked me why I thought the plane was flying upside down. Maybe all the flips crossed some wires in his head."

I jumped when the phone rang again a minute later. I was afraid to answer it and start another odd conversation with Grandpa.

"Hello?"

"So, you *are* home." This time, it was Mom and she sounded mad. "Mister, you're in big trouble!"

"Hi, Mom. What's wrong?"

"What's wrong? I'll tell you what's wrong. I just got a call from your school telling me that you and Emily haven't been there all week. And now, it's after 8 o'clock on Thursday when you should be in school and you're still home!"

"Huh?"

"Don't try to play cute with me, young man. The principal also told me that you're going to fail science for the marking period because you skipped your weather test."

"I what?"

"You heard me. Just because I've had to work a couple of day shifts doesn't mean that you can do whatever you want. I really thought you were more responsible than that, David. I'm VERY disappointed in you. And, I'm pretty sure your sister didn't get the idea to skip school on her own, but now she's done it, too. Thanks to you, you are both grounded."

"We're what?" This conversation was even stranger than the one with Grandpa.

"Let me spell it for you...G-R-O-U-N-D-E-D. And just in case you missed a spelling test too, that spells GROUNDED!"

"I don't understand...Did they take away the snow cancellation for today?"

"David, we haven't had snow in over two weeks. Now stop all this silliness and get to school."

"No snow? But, Mom, it's been snowing for like five days. It just stopped this morning. Don't you remember calling me about it an hour ago?"

"Is that supposed to be an insanity plea? Now you're really pushing the limits."

I was so confused. Were Mom and Grandpa playing a joke on me to get back at me for using the Snowmallows? If they were, Mom should have been an actress instead of a doctor.

"Can we still go for a walk after school?" I asked.

"No, we cannot! Grounded does not mean you are free to walk about the grounds. I'm going to hang up now before they admit me for hypertension. You and your sister get to school – NOW!"

"We will, Mom, I promise, but, before you hang up, I need to tell you that Grandpa called. He wants you to pick him up at Terminal 2 in an hour."

"Thank you for passing along the message. Now go to school." Mom hanging up on me proved there would be no other questions or negotiations.

I stared at the phone receiver in disbelief. "We really need to get caller ID on this phone. I'm afraid to answer it."

"What happened?" Emily asked.

I hung the receiver up carefully. "We're grounded for skipping school all week. Mom is furious. I don't understand what's going on."

Snowball jumped on a chair and sat with his back to the phone as if shunning Mom for yelling at me.

"That doesn't make any sense. How could we go to school in a snowstorm?" Jon asked. He sounded like his head was getting stuffier.

"According to Mom, we never had a storm. I'm not sure what's happening, but I think we'd better get to school before we get in more trouble."

CHAPTER 19

Thursday, March 7 – During School

J ust like the phone calls that morning, it turned out to be an odd day at school.

"Where were you all week?" Cassie asked.

"Did you go on vacation?" asked Evan.

"Did you catch some horrible disease that your parents brought home from the hospital?" Drama covered his nose and mouth with his sleeve as he talked. "Does Jon have the same thing? Is that why he keeps sneezing?"

The only answer I could give anyone was "no". What else was I going to say? No one seemed to remember the snowstorm at all. The Snowmallow problem clearly wasn't solved.

Unfortunately, neither was the problem of the weather test. And, now, it was Jon's problem, too.

Along with my family, Ms. Fredericks had the office call his family about missing school and the test.

"But, Ms. Fredericks, why can't we take a makeup test?" I asked.

"We really do know the material," added Jon.

Ms. Fredericks frowned and shook her head. "I'm sorry, boys. I could've given you one if your parents had excused your absence. But, since they didn't, I'm not allowed to give you a makeup test. It's one of the bigger punishments for skipping school." She started walking back to her desk, then paused and looked back at us. "It's too bad. You're both normally such responsible young men. I really wish things were different."

I felt the same way. If things were different, Jon and I wouldn't be sinking back into our chairs in defeat.

Thankfully, there was one thing in our favor today. Thursday was library day. As soon as we got to the library, Jon and I hurried to one of the computers in a hidden corner. I hopped onto the internet and brought up the local news site to see if there was any information on what had happened the past week.

I whispered to Jon. "That's strange. There's nothing on any local news sites about snow at all. In fact, Brian the Meteorologist has an article posted about the unseasonably warm weather we've had all week. The last snowstorm reported was the one from two weeks ago. It was the storm he said was going to be bad and then we only got a couple of inches."

"Look at this." Jon pointed to some information in the sidebar. "It looks like the weather's been so warm and dry for the past week that there are actually fire danger areas showing on the weather map. And, look at the allergy levels. They're sky high."

Jon rubbed his red, sticky eyes.

Ms. Fredericks came around the corner. She seemed surprised to see us. "What are you two doing hiding back here in the corner? Do I need to worry about you skipping out again?"

"No, Ms. Fredericks," I said. "We're not going anywhere."

"We're just researching current events," said Jon.

"That's good," she said. Ms. Fredericks stood on her toes and scanned the room. "Actually, I was looking for Drama – I mean Henry. Have either of you seen him?"

The sound of a crash on the other side of the library got her attention.

"Never mind." She rushed toward the noise.

"Current events. Good cover," I said to Jon.

"It's true," he said.

"Got any other good ideas for figuring out what's going on?"

"Why don't we do a search for recent large storms and see what comes up? Maybe somebody else reported on the snow?"

I typed "recent storms" into the search engine and hit enter. A long list of articles popped up about earthquakes and tornado threats, but not the recent record snow that buried Connecticut. As we scrolled through the list, one article finally appeared that was titled "Snowstorm Blankets New England".

"It's from a newspaper in Arizona," I said. "Why is there only one article and why is it from way out in Arizona?"

"Got me, Dave. Let's print it."

"You have fifteen minutes left of library time," Ms. Fredericks told the class. "Please check out any books you need and line up near the door when you're done."

I hit print and Jon went to the printer to pick up the article. It didn't make any sense to me. Why Arizona? I quickly did a search of library books that gave information about different U.S. states. I rushed to the shelf where they were kept and picked out one called *50 State Nuggets – Valuable Facts about the U.S. State by State*. I checked it out at the circulation desk and got in line at the door just as Ms. Fredericks was telling us to head back to our classroom.

*

At the end of the school day, Jon and I picked up Emily at her classroom.

"How was your day?" I asked.

"That was the weirdest day of school ever. Everyone wanted to know where I was all week. Was I sick? Was I on vacation? Then Ryan Redmond told me he missed me – ick! And now I've got a ton of homework and the teacher is mad at me. It was awful. It's like no one remembers the past week except us."

"Sounds like someone has an admirer," teased Jon. His voice was nasal, like he had come down with a bad cold. "Do you need me to talk to this Redmond kid for you?"

Emily's face grimaced and she made a small gagging noise. "I don't even want to think about that. My day has been bad enough. David, what's going on?"

"I don't know, Em, but Arizona might have an answer."

My sister shook her head at me. "Oh, no. We're not running away to Arizona, are we?"

"Not if we can help it," I said. "Jon and I found an article from Arizona on the internet that might give us some answers."

Jon pulled a folded sheet of paper out of his pocket and began reading the article to us.

"Snowstorm Blankets New England"

Thursday, March 7 – 6:00am MST

As they say in New England, if you don't like the weather, wait a minute. That phrase rung true as a surprise snowstorm blanketed the State of Connecticut in over six-and-a-half feet of the white stuff over the past five days. Most of the snow fell from Tuesday night through the course of the day on Wednesday, many times causing white out conditions. However, just as they were starting to call neighboring states asking for trucks and line crews to assist with the cleanup, the storm stopped, and the snow completely evaporated as quickly and unexpectedly as it started. There is still no explanation for what caused the storm or its equally unlikely end. Follow up calls made after the storm to contacts in New England were odd also. Most folks acted as if no snow had fallen. Considering all this mystery, we in Arizona will take the dry heat any day.

"And there were no other articles anywhere about it?" asked Emily.

Jon folded up the paper. "Not that we found – not even any local ones."

Emily scratched her head. "What does it mean?"

"I don't know, Em, but I'm going to find out," I said. I took the article from Jon and slid it into my backpack. "This is my mess, so you guys shouldn't get in trouble for it."

As we approached the house, Grandpa was sitting on the front porch steps. Emily ran to him. Now I knew what we needed to do next.

"You know what, Jon? I think it might be time for me to talk about the weather with Grandpa."

"I thought you said that was more boring than a rain delay at a major league game. Besides, he can't tell you about what happened this week. He doesn't remember it either."

"I know. But he will be able to tell me more about the Snowmallows. Hopefully, I can figure it out from there."

CHAPTER 20

Thursday, March 7 – After School

We caught up with Emily who stood next to the porch steps. Grandpa sat on the top step of the porch with a big, yellow bucket of clean water on one side of him and a stack of dirty equipment and camping gear on the other. He was wiping it all down but stopped briefly when he saw Jon and me.

"Hi, Doctor Wilson. Welcome home." Jon pulled out a tissue.

"Hello, Jon. Nice to be home." Grandpa grimaced a little when he heard Jon blow his nose. "You don't sound so good. Got a change of season cold?"

Jon rubbed his eyes with the back of his hand. "No, sir, just allergies."

"I hear you. Hope you feel better." Grandpa turned to me. "Hello, David, how are you?"

"Hi, Grandpa. I'm fine. How was your trip?"

Grandpa turned back to cleaning a large metal clip. "It was good. I was just telling Emily that I have a couple of souvenirs for you from my layover in Chile, but your Mom says I can't give them to you." Grandpa lifted his eyes and peered at me over the top of his glasses. His eyebrow was raised in a quizzical look. "Something about you being grounded for skipping school?"

Emily and Jon stared down at the ground. I kept eye contact with Grandpa but didn't say anything. I wasn't sure if I wanted to answer.

Grandpa lowered his eyes and continued polishing the clip. "You know, it's one thing not to tell anyone where you've been before you get caught skipping school, but after you're caught – that's another matter entirely."

"It's a long story and I'm not sure how to explain it," I answered.

Grandpa held the clip up to the light, gave it one last wipe, and set it down behind his back with some other clean equipment. Then he looked me in the eye and gave me an understanding smile. "Sounds intriguing," he said. Then he took a metal spike from the dirty pile and brushed some excess dirt off it. "Well, when you figure it out, I'll be happy to listen. I've had lots of things happen in my life that I can't explain either."

Grandpa's answer and the understanding look surprised me. "Really? Like what?" I asked.

"Well, for starters, I'm a weather scientist in Connecticut. That alone provides plenty of things I can't explain."

"Preachin' to the choir," said Jon. I coughed and gave him a "be quiet" look. Jon went back to staring at the ground.

"What else can't you explain, Grandpa?" asked Emily. She sat on the step below him.

"Oh, lots of things." He began washing the metal spike. "Like how I could be lucky enough to meet and marry your Grandmother or how blessed we were to have your mother as our daughter. Sometimes I wonder why Grandma had to be in that accident and how I can miss her so much." Grandpa looked up at Emily and changed his serious look to a smile. "And, of course, I wonder how I ended up with the best grandkids ever." He gave Emily a quick tap on the nose with his finger that made her laugh.

I hadn't seen that playful side of Grandpa since the day we dyed marshmallows in the lab. In fact, seeing it now made me even more worried that the plane flying upside down really did scramble something in his brain. The only problem with that theory was that Emily didn't seem surprised by this side of him.

"Tell us a story about Grandma," said Emily. "I don't remember her."

"Let's see..."

Grandpa stopped washing and closed his eyes as if he was trying to think back over the stories in his head.

"Tell us the one about how you got her to marry you," said Emily. "That's my favorite."

"You've heard that one so many times, though," Grandpa answered.

I had no idea what story they were talking about, so how could Emily have heard it over and over?

"I've never heard it," I said.

Grandpa opened his eyes and did the peering over the glasses thing again. "Really?"

Emily made a pleading face. "Please. For David."

"If you insist," said Grandpa. "I have to admit that one's my favorite, too."

Emily gave a little clap with her hands.

Jon and I sat down on the porch steps next to her, so we were all at Grandpa's feet. Snowball wandered out from under a bush and rubbed on the garden gnome he'd wrestled earlier in the day. Then the cat climbed the porch stairs and waited for Grandpa to set down his work before stepping onto his lap. Grandpa scratched the kitty behind the ears and started his story.

"For starters, your Grandma was beautiful both inside and out and could have dated any man she wanted."

I thought back to pictures of my Grandmother when she was young. It always struck me that someone so pretty could wind up with a strange guy like Grandpa.

"She was from Florida and I was from Connecticut," he continued. "When I was a senior in college, I was sent to Florida for a six-month internship to study hurricane patterns. At first, I hated it down there. It was summer, and it was too hot and humid for me, but one night, some friends invited me to join them at a beach party. There were people there playing volleyball, other people walking out into the surf, and more people talking and eating and laughing. My friends kept wandering off as they saw other people they knew, so before long, I was sitting on a beach blanket next to the campfire by myself. I didn't mind, though, because it gave me a chance to people-watch. I was shy back then, so it was usually easier for me to watch people than it was for me to talk to them."

So that was why Grandpa spent so much time alone in his lab or off collecting stuff in jars. I never thought about him being shy.

"Anyway," said Grandpa, "I sat by the campfire and scanned the crowd. There were lots of interesting people to watch, but then I saw HER..."

"Who?" said Emily.

"Who do you think?" asked Grandpa.

"Grandma!" Emily had a giddy-looking smile on her face.

"Of course." Grandpa got the same giddy-looking smile. "I couldn't take my eyes off her. She was the most beautiful person I'd ever seen and lots of people were coming over to talk to her."

"What did you do?" Jon asked.

Grandpa sighed. "I just sat there. I figured with all the athletic guys around her that a science guy like me didn't stand a chance anyway. So, I just continued to people watch and tried not to be too obvious about the fact that I was mostly watching her. I think I did a pretty bad job of that because, before long, she came over to me."

"Was she mad at you for staring at her?" I asked.

"No. She was sweet. I think she felt sorry for me. She said, 'Are you here all by yourself?' And I said, 'Nope. There's a hermit crab right over there. See it?'"

* 165 *

I shook my head in disbelief. "Seriously, Grandpa? That's the first thing you said to the prettiest girl you ever saw?"

"I'm afraid so. I told you I was better at watching people than talking to them. Fortunately, she laughed and asked if she could sit down, so it worked out. She had some marshmallows and some sticks to toast them on, so we sat by the campfire on the blanket and talked and toasted marshmallows. She was so pretty and confident that when she sat down, it made me nervous and I almost couldn't look at her." Grandpa laughed. "But I got over that quickly because she made it very easy to talk to her."

"What did you talk about?" Emily asked.

"Believe it or not, she was happy talking about the weather. She was interested in what I did and in what Connecticut was like. I told her all the things I liked about the weather up here, especially the snow. She told me that she'd never seen real snow and that some time she was going to go somewhere where she could have a real white Christmas. I knew right then that she was the girl for me, and I made a plan to give her that white Christmas."

For once, Grandpa's story held my attention. It wasn't because I needed his help. It was because I was interested in the story – in this side of my grandparents that I never knew.

"Over the next few months," Grandpa continued, "we went out together almost every day. My internship was ending around Thanksgiving and a few weeks before that, I launched my plan to marry her. I invited her to come to Connecticut for Christmas and I guaranteed her that there would be snow for her. I told her that we didn't always get a white Christmas, but for her, I'd make sure it happened. She laughed and said, 'If you make sure I see real snow for Christmas, I'll marry you.' That was all I needed to hear."

"Wasn't that kind of a big chance to take?" Jon asked. "I mean, you said yourself the weather up here is unpredictable. What if it didn't snow?"

"Well, I admit it was risky. But she was worth it, and I had a plan. I was a little homesick when I first got to Florida, so I made a list of things I liked about winter to make me feel closer to home. I decided to use that list to help me develop a formula for creating snow that I could test when I got home. My parents helped me set up the weather lab in the basement so I could work there when I returned. My biggest concern was that I would have trouble finding the components I needed for my formula. Fortunately, we had a week of really severe winter weather right after I got back."

"How was bad weather fortunate?" I asked.

Grandpa scratched Snowball under the chin. "It was fortunate because it allowed me to collect lots of the great winter weather items I needed – things like blizzard winds and charcoal dust from snowman eyes. But, even when I had those things, it wasn't easy. I worked for three weeks straight until I finally had the formula just right. I mixed it together and put it inside some marshmallows that I'd cut to look like snowflakes. I thought she'd like that since we toasted marshmallows that first time we met."

Blizzard winds...charcoal dust from Snowman's eyes...marshmallows shaped like snowflakes. I finally connected the dots in my head and listened intently as Grandpa continued.

"By then it was mid-December, and Grandma was making her final plans to visit me. It was unseasonably warm up here the week before Christmas, so there was no snow. All of us meteorologists knew there wasn't a snowflake's chance at the Equator of seeing a white Christmas. But your Grandmother came up from Florida on Christmas Eve, anyway. I picked her up at the airport and I could see she was disappointed that there wasn't any snow. That made me smile because I knew then that she really did want to marry me. In fact, she got angry with me that I was so happy, but I had a plan." Grandpa gave a sly wink to Emily. Emily gave him that giddy smile again.

"We drove back to the house and had dinner with my parents. They loved your grandma the moment they met her. After dinner, I said, 'Why don't I show you the lab and we can have some cocoa and talk?' She said, 'Sure.' So, I made one mug of cocoa and escorted her downstairs."

"One mug?" asked Jon. "Why only one?"

"She asked the same thing," said Grandpa. "I told her she'd see in a minute. So, we went downstairs. I had the lab all decorated in twinkly lights and had Christmas music playing. I put the mug on the lab table and handed her a ring box wrapped in silver paper. She opened it and found one of the marshmallow snowflakes inside. She said, 'You know this doesn't count as real snow, right?' And I said, 'It will.' Then I dropped the snowflake into the mug. The cocoa started to fizz and, a few seconds later, it was flurrying on top of our heads. Her mouth dropped open in surprise and she looked up at the ceiling. Then, she stuck out her tongue to try to catch some of the snowflakes. I took her by the hand and got down on one knee as the snow fell softly on us. I pulled a diamond ring out of my pocket and I said, 'I made it snow for Christmas. You know what that means, right?' She said, 'Yes.' And, the rest, as they say, is history."

"How did you get it to stop snowing?" asked Emily.

"It stopped on its own after about five minutes. I didn't use very much formula that first time, so it didn't last long.

"I can't believe I never heard that story," I said softly. With the past week's events, it was a lot to process.

"And that's why you bring a mug of cocoa to the lab every Christmas Eve, right?" Emily asked.

"Yes," Grandpa said. "It became Grandma's and my special tradition to use the Snowmallows every year on Christmas Eve. Snowmallows – that's the name she gave them. After that first year, we set up the weather locker so we wouldn't have to clean the snow out of the lab. That was a good thing, too, because the second year we had two mugs of cocoa, so it snowed a lot longer."

"I don't mean to be disrespectful, but wouldn't she be more impressed if you made it snow outside?" asked Jon.

"Maybe, but the Snowmallows were never stable enough to expose to the outside air. There's no telling what might've happened if they mixed with another weather pattern."

"So, you've never, ever used them outside?" I asked.

"No." A smirk crossed Grandpa's face. "Why? Do you need a snow day to catch up on all the work you missed?"

I smiled weakly. "No, we'll get caught up on our own. Thanks for the story, Grandpa. It was great."

"It's too bad you couldn't experiment with time and weather," said Emily. "Maybe you could go back and see Grandma again."

"You know, Emily, sometimes I wonder, 'Would I change anything if I could do it all again?' For example, maybe if we'd lived in Florida instead of Connecticut, Grandma wouldn't have gotten into her accident, but then I realize that our lives would be very different if things didn't happen as they did."

I wasn't sure what he was getting at. "What do you mean?"

Grandpa lifted Snowball off his lap and put him down on the top step next to his clean gear. Grandpa rubbed his leg and stretched it out. "I believe that things happen for a reason, David.

Did you know that your mother wasn't always a trauma surgeon?"

"She wasn't?" said Emily.

"No," Grandpa answered. "She was an internist before the accident, but she became a trauma surgeon after your Grandma passed so that she could help other accident victims. Just think how many people have been helped by that choice alone."

Grandpa's words made me pause. I remembered Mom going back to school for a little while after the accident, but never realized why. And I never thought about my parents making choices about their jobs. I knew what they did, but never thought about why they did it.

"No," Grandpa continued, "it's best to leave things like time and weather to powers greater than us."

"Do you mean God?" asked Emily.

Grandpa picked up his washing cloth and another metal spike. "Yes, I would say that God is a power greater than us."

My head was already swimming with new information about my grandparents, but this comment about God really threw me. "Are you saying you believe in God?" I asked.

"Sure," answered Grandpa.

"But you're a scientist."

Grandpa smiled. "The two aren't mutually exclusive, David. You can be a person of faith and a person of science."

"My Dad told me that there were a lot of great scientists in history who believed in God," said Jon.

"That's true," said Grandpa. "There are even people today who feel science supports faith. It helps them see God's hand in creation."

I took a minute to think about it. Maybe those people had God moments, too.

"Look, David," said Grandpa. "All I'm saying is that there are some things like time and weather that we should deal with carefully. Playing around with either is dangerous enough, but, combining the two – that could be a recipe for disaster. Time is too fragile and important a gift to be used for something selfish."

Suddenly my shoulders felt heavy again. "Speaking of time, we'd better get started on all that homework. Thanks again, Grandpa."

As Jon, Emily, and I went inside, Jon said what I was thinking. "I don't like what your Grandpa said about mixing time and weather, especially since we were messing around with clocks this morning."

We heard the door to the upstairs apartment open. Mrs. Strong called down to us. "Jonathan Peter Strong, is that you? Get up here right now, please. You have some explaining to do before I decide how long to ground you."

Jon winced. "Guess I'd better go."

"Sounds that way," I said. "Don't worry. I'll check the Arizona info tonight. We'll talk about it tomorrow on the way to school."

Jon nodded, turned slowly, and trudged up the stairs.

CHAPTER 21

Thursday, March 7 – Late Afternoon

Emily and I headed to the kitchen to get a snack. I grabbed an apple and went to the sink to wash it. Emily grabbed a Bunny's Best Marshmallow Rabbit from a package on the counter. I took it out of her hands before it got to her mouth. "Don't eat those, Em. We might need them. Besides, haven't you had enough of them this week?"

Emily gave me a blank stare. "I don't know what you're talking about. I don't remember..."

I shook my finger back and forth at her. "Don't pretend you forgot what happened this week so you can eat one of those. I know you remember."

I handed her the clean apple. Emily sighed and took the apple to her room. I washed another one for me and headed to my room.

As I dropped my backpack on the twin bed that Emily used, I realized that both beds were still unmade. I straightened them out quickly. I certainly didn't need another reason to be grounded.

When I was done, I pulled out the library book and the internet article. I took a bite of my apple, sat down on my bed, and re-read the article a few times. Unfortunately, I didn't get any new information. Next, I grabbed the *50 State Nuggets* book. I flipped to the section about Arizona and read it. There was information about the state capital (Phoenix), the state bird (the cactus wren), and the state flower (the saguaro cactus blossom). I read about the Grand Canyon and other parks and natural sights. There was even information on copper mines. But, as far as I could tell, none of this helped explain why Arizona was the only place that knew about the snowstorm. If anything, when I read about their normal weather patterns, it didn't seem like most parts of Arizona would know much about large snowstorms at all. Then, just as I was about to give up, I read something interesting:

"Much of Arizona remains on Mountain Standard Time year-round. Due to the high heat during the sunlit hours of the day, many activities begin after dark. Therefore, there is no benefit in most of the state to observing Daylight Saving Time. As a result, most of the state opted out of the national requirement to turn their clocks ahead one hour in the spring and back one hour in the fall…"

Could that have something to do with it? I finished the apple and went back to the kitchen to throw out the core. Emily was already there doing the same thing.

"I'm not sure, but I think I might have found something," I whispered.

"Really? What is it?"

Emily followed me to my room. I showed her what I read in the Arizona book.

"What's Daylight Saving Time?" she asked.

"I'm not exactly sure. It has something to do with changing the clocks at certain times of the year to give more daylight hours. You know that thing that Mom always says whenever we have to do it – Spring Forward, Fall Backward."

"I remember that saying. And, I think that's this weekend," said Emily.

"How do you know that?"

"When you and Jon were outside shoveling and Mrs. Strong and I were making cookies, there was something on the TV to remind people that it was coming up this weekend. I think they were afraid with all the other stuff going on that people would forget about it. Mrs. Strong wrote herself a note that said, 'Spring Forward – March 10'. She said she didn't want them to miss church because she forgot to change the clocks."

"That might be important," I said. "Em, do you think when I turned the clocks around this morning that I could've messed up time for everyone except the places where they don't change their clocks?"

She shrugged her shoulders. "Maybe." Emily was silent for a moment as if she had something else to say but wasn't sure if I'd like it.

"What is it, Em?" I asked.

"I think we should tell Grandpa about what happened. I don't know if he'll believe us, but, if he does, maybe he can help."

"Actually, I was thinking the same thing. We may be in more trouble for being in the lab without him," I said. "But, after what he said about mixing time and weather, I think we're in trouble up to our ears already. I think he's the only one who can help us."

Emily looked relieved that I agreed. "Can we go see him now?"

"Why wait?" I stuck the Arizona article in my pocket. "As Grandpa said, 'Time is fragile' so let's not waste it."

CHAPTER 22

Thursday, March 7 – Before Dinner

When we got to the lab, we found Grandpa sorting his clean gear on the black-topped table. Snowball was standing next to some jars of his samples, sniffing them and rubbing his face against them.

We weren't even all the way through the doorway before he spoke. "Shouldn't you two be in your rooms?" asked Grandpa. "You know the word 'grounded' doesn't mean you're free to walk about the grounds."

I wondered how he knew we were there. He wasn't even looking in our direction. I tried not to seem nervous, but my hands were shaking.

"We know, Grandpa, and we're sorry, but Em and I wanted to talk to you about something important. We think you might be the only one who will understand."

"Sounds serious." Grandpa stopped sorting. "Does this have anything to do with where you've been all week?"

I nodded.

Grandpa gestured for us to come to the black-topped table. "Have a seat and tell me what's on your mind."

Emily and I sat on the tall stools while Grandpa cleared a space at the table in front of us. Grandpa sat too, and I told him the same story I told him on the phone that morning. The only difference was that this time I gave him all the details including everything that had happened since turning the bird clock back an hour. Last, I pulled the Arizona article out of my pocket and showed it to him.

Grandpa read the article. He set it down on the table, stared up at the ceiling, and rubbed his chin with his hand as if he was deep in thought. Then he got up, went to his desk, and picked up a box that was sitting on top of it. "That would explain why all of this stuff was sitting on the table when I got back to the lab today."

He showed us the contents of the box. At the top of the pile were two baseball gloves and some car wash sponges.

"Our spring stuff!" cried Emily.

"After Mom called this morning, we got dressed and went right to school. We never got back down here to clean up the lab." I grabbed my glove out of the box. It was like seeing an old friend. "So, does this mean you believe us?" I asked.

"Yes, David, I do. This box and the fact that, when I got home, the time on my phone and my watch didn't agree to any of the clocks in the lab makes me believe that something strange happened here. I was also wondering why my chili pepper allergy has been acting up all day."

Grandpa rolled up his sleeve to reveal a few splotchy red patches on his arm.

"Sorry about that, Grandpa," said Emily.

"And about the mess in the lab and for using the Snowmallows," I added. "I never thought it would cause all this trouble."

"I know. And I can tell that you really did try to fix things. I'm proud of you for that, but I wish you'd told me the truth sooner. We could've been working on a solution already."

I felt a sudden burst of hope. "You'll help us?" I asked.

"Well, I have to admit that the scientist in me is curious."

Emily clapped. "Hooray!"

She threw her arms around his neck and gave him a big hug. He gave her a big hug back. I thanked Grandpa, but I didn't hug him. I wasn't sure if I should.

Grandpa took my glove and put it back in the box of spring items. Then he put the box back on his desk. "Don't thank me yet. We have work to do. You know, I went to Antarctica to try to develop ways to make winter storms easier here. I was just hoping to find faster, better ways to get ice off roads and roofs. But with what you've done, we may have all kinds of weather possibilities. You may be more of a scientist than you think, David."

Maybe I was wrong. Maybe talking weather with Grandpa wasn't that bad.

"So, where do we start?" I asked.

Grandpa looked between his watch and one of the clocks in the lab. "It's almost dinner time – or at least I think it is if I set my watch correctly. Let's eat first. While we eat, we'll need to convince your parents to let you help me in the lab tonight."

I nodded. "Don't worry, Grandpa. I know just what to do."

CHAPTER 23

Thursday, March 7 – Dinner

Dinner wound down just as Grandpa finished telling us about his trip.

"It sounds like you had a really productive time," said my Mom. "Don't you think so, David?"

I answered Mom with a bored "Mm-hmm" while I poked my fork at the remaining broccoli on my plate.

"David, have you even been listening?" asked Dad. "You've been staring at your plate all through dinner as if steamed broccoli and grilled chicken was the most interesting thing at the table."

"Mm-hmm."

Dad raised his voice. "David!"

I jumped as if he startled me and looked up from my plate. "What's the matter, Dad?" I asked.

Mom rolled her eyes. "Well, I'm glad your Grandfather had a great trip and I'm glad he's safely back at home."

"Thanks. I really did enjoy it," Grandpa said. "But I can't believe how much gear I still have to unpack before I can start working with my data. There's stuff all over the lab."

Dad shook his head. "I have paperwork to do tonight and late meetings tomorrow, but I can help you over the weekend."

"I'm in the same boat," Mom added.

"Thank you for the offer, but I can't wait until the weekend. I want to work with the data while it's fresh in my head," said Grandpa. "At my age, I can't delay like I used to!"

Mom laughed. "Don't sell yourself short. You're still young." She patted Grandpa gently on the shoulder. Then I saw a familiar gleam in her eye. "Hey, I have an idea. Maybe David can help you unpack your gear."

I gave her a look like she was crazy. "Wait, what? You want me to help Grandpa?"

She frowned at me. "Yes, I think it'd be good for you to help your Grandfather unpack his gear."

"Seriously?" I made sure to sound really upset with the idea. "Come on, Mom. I'm already grounded. Isn't that enough punishment?"

Dad's scowled at me. "David, that was disrespectful and I'm disappointed in you. Apologize to your Grandfather right now."

"Sorry, Grandpa." I used the same tone of voice as I did with the "Mm-hmm's".

"Don't worry about it, David," said Grandpa. "Maybe grilled chicken and steamed broccoli are more interesting than me sometimes. But I really can use the help."

"It's settled then," said Mom. "David, you'll go help Grandpa in the lab tonight. He needs you and, from your tone, it sounds like a good addition to your punishment – no offense Dad."

Grandpa laughed. "None taken."

"Aw, man." I got up from the table and put my plate in the sink.

"As a matter of fact," Mom continued, "I'm going to send a text to Tess Strong to see if Jon can help, too."

She went to the living room to get her phone.

"Can I help, too, Daddy?" Emily asked.

"I don't know, Em. Being in the lab might be too much fun for you while you're grounded. I know you like it down there."

"Actually, it might help to have at least one willing participant," said Grandpa. "Don't worry, I won't make it too much fun."

Dad chuckled. "In that case, you can go, Em."

Mom came back from the living room. "Jon's in. He'll meet you in the lab in half an hour."

"Sounds like a plan," said Grandpa.

Dad stood up from the table and picked up his plate. "Let's clean up these dishes so you guys can get started."

As Mom put the leftovers in the fridge and Dad started washing dishes, I looked over at Grandpa and mouthed the words, "It worked."

Grandpa gave me a wink and took some dirty plates to the sink. I thought for a moment that if the time shift never got fixed and I wasn't ever allowed to play baseball again, I could become a stage actor.

*

When dinner was over and the dishes were cleaned up, Grandpa, Emily, Snowball, and I met Jon in the lab. To our surprise, Deacon Strong was there, too.

"I thought another strong body might be helpful – no pun intended," said Deacon Strong.

Grandpa laughed, but Jon didn't.

Deacon Strong held up a plate full of thick brownies. The smell of warm chocolate filled the room. "A welcome home gift from my wife. Made with her special recipe. She puts extra chocolate bits in them to make them extra gooey. Jon likes them that way."

"Thank you. That was very thoughtful of her. How did she bake them so quickly? Audra only called her a little while ago."

"She knew you were coming back today and planned to make them for you. She started them before your daughter called us for help," said

Deacon Strong. "This just turned out to be a good excuse for delivering them."

"Please tell her they look delicious. Would you like one?" Grandpa asked.

"No, thanks." Deacon Strong patted his stomach. "If I ate everything Tess made, I'd be twice the man I am today."

"I understand." Grandpa cleared a place on the lab table for the plate of brownies. "Marie, my wife, was a good cook, too. I've lost a few pounds since she's been gone."

"Did you have a good trip?"

As Grandpa chatted with Deacon Strong about his work, Jon walked over to where Emily and I were standing. He looked worried and tired. I was sure being grounded was a new experience for him. I also knew that Jon was close to his parents, so keeping the truth from them couldn't be easy, either.

"Are you all right?" I whispered.

"No. How are we supposed to fix whatever's going on if your grandpa's in our main workspace? I've been trying to figure that out all afternoon."

"Relax, Jon. Em and I talked to him. Grandpa knows what happened and he's going to help us."

"Really? Well, that's good." Jon's frown softened a little. "Now, what do we do about Dad? He thinks we're here to clean up the lab and he wants to help."

I smiled and put a hand on Jon's shoulder. "Maybe we should tell him, too."

Jon's shoulders, which looked like they were holding up his ears, suddenly dropped to their normal position. "Could we? Do you think he'll believe us?"

I nodded. "Yes. Grandpa does, so I think he will, too. Besides, your dad needs to know that you didn't do anything wrong. The past week was my fault."

Emily pointed toward the door. "Well, if you're going to tell him, you'd better do it fast."

Grandpa was shaking hands with Deacon Strong and leading him to the door. "Thanks for offering to help, Mike, but I'll be fine with just the children. Please thank Tess for the brownies, and for letting me borrow Jon."

"Wait!" said Jon and I at the same time.

Grandpa and Deacon Strong paused at the door. "What's the matter, boys?" asked Grandpa while he gave me the over the glasses look.

Jon walked over to his father. He led him to one of the stools and pulled it out for him. "Dad, there's something I need to tell you."

Deacon Strong raised a nervous looking eyebrow. "I'm not sure if it's good news when you start off that way, son."

"Well, it's good and bad," I said. "Good because you'll know where we've been all week and bad...well...for the same reason."

"You know, Doc," Deacon Strong said to Grandpa, "I think I will take one of those brownies. I have a feeling I'm going to need the sustenance."

Grandpa handed him two brownies on a paper towel. "Take two. It's a long story."

For the third time that day, I recounted the story of the past week. I paused this time to answer questions from Grandpa. He took careful notes about the times of day that things occurred, the quantities of ingredients we used, and other specific details that might help solve the problem.

Jon and Emily jumped in where they thought I might be missing a piece of the story.

Throughout the story, Deacon Strong listened quietly. At the end, the two brownies were still on the paper towel in front of him and he didn't say anything for several minutes.

Finally, Jon waved his hand in front of his father's face as if to pull him out of a trance. "Dad, are you there?"

"Yes," said Deacon Strong. "But, for the last few minutes, I've been trying to remember what I did this past week and I can't. It was all so clear upstairs, but now...all I know is that my muscles ache a lot. They ache like they do when I move a lot of snow."

"The lab seems to be immune from the time shift," explained Grandpa. "It's specially insulated so that what happens in here doesn't impact the outside weather and vice versa. That may be why last week seems a little fuzzy to you. The timeline in here was never adjusted, so your mind may be trying to shift your memory back to what really happened. In my case, I've been having visions all afternoon of flying upside down in a plane." Grandpa shuddered at the thought.

Deacon Strong grimaced. "I would NOT like that."

"Tell me about it," said Grandpa.

Jon looked anxiously between the two men like he was watching the match point at a tennis game. Finally, he blurted out, "Dad, do you believe us?"

Deacon Strong smiled at him. "The Lord said, 'Blessed are they who have not seen, but believe'. Looks like I'm going to have to take you at your word."

Jon hugged his father. "Thanks, Dad."

"You're welcome, son," he said returning the hug. "Now, tell me. How can I help?"

CHAPTER 24

Thursday, March 7 – After Dinner

"**I** think we need to start by doing what your parents think you're doing," said Grandpa. "It's a mess in here."

"At least that way we aren't lying," said Jon. I was glad to see Jon was back to normal.

Snowball tiptoed in and around the piles of Grandpa's stuff, sniffing it curiously but cautiously. As Grandpa carefully unpacked his boxes and bags, he sorted the items into piles on the black-topped table depending on where in the lab they belonged. Jon put samples onto the shelves along the walls. Deacon Strong helped Emily put away pieces of equipment since she already knew where most of them belonged but couldn't reach all the places. And I took care of putting away the books and notebooks that belonged on the shelves above the desk. I tried not to kick up too much dust as I worked.

Things moved along quickly, except for Jon who kept stopping to read the labels on the jars of samples before putting them away. Jon said it was to make sure he put like items together, but I suspected, that after the past several days, Jon was also interested in what was in them. I had to admit that I was curious, too. So, when I finished putting away the books, I helped Jon with the samples. I counted twenty-five jars labeled "Antarctic Polar Wind – use insulated gloves when opening", twenty labeled "Melted Antarctic Ice – use polar wind to reconstitute", and five labeled "Southern Elephant Seal Pod Scent".

"Grandpa," I asked. "Why are there only five for the scent of the elephant seals?"

Grandpa gave his nose a quick pinch. "If you'd ever smelled a pod of elephant seals, you'd understand."

The last group of jars made Jon's eyes light up. There were four jars labeled "Loose Feathers – Snow Petrel", fifteen labeled "Emperor Penguins

Calls", and ten labeled "Emperor Penguin Water Splashes." Snowball seemed almost as excited as Jon as he sniffed the jars vigorously.

"Doctor Wilson," Jon asked Grandpa. "Are these sounds from real Emperor Penguins?"

"They certainly are. I find it always helps to have the real sound of something for a formula. It gives a more precise result."

I put the last jar on the shelf. "That's part of our problem, isn't it? Using the clock sounds wasn't as good as using the sound of a real bird, right?"

"Maybe," replied Grandpa. "We'll have to do some tests to figure that out."

I looked around the room. Deacon Strong was breaking down the last of the empty boxes and Emily folded and put away the last empty bag.

"Nice job, everyone. Thanks for the help," said Grandpa.

"What's next?" I asked.

"Now we start on the Snowmallow problem. Let's look at what we have and figure out if we need anything else."

Grandpa put the notebook with the Snowmallow formula and the bag of Snowmallows onto the empty table. Then he put the box of spring items next to that. "Jon, Emily, and David, you're up. Show me your stuff," said Grandpa.

Emily got a couple of old mugs off one of the shelves while Jon and I began unpacking the box of spring items and spreading things out on the table.

"Looks like they've done this before," said Deacon Strong about all the activity around him.

Grandpa nodded. "I'd say so. They're like a well-oiled machine."

Snowball wandered from the fishy-smelling jars on the shelves to the middle of the table. Emily gave him a scratch behind the ears. He peeked over the side of the box of spring things and jumped in it as we were still trying to unpack it. He pawed at our fingers as we pulled the last few needed items from the box. Then he shoved himself in between the DVD's and pictures left in the bottom and put his head down for a nap.

Jon stared at the cat wedged between the DVD's. "What is wrong with this cat?"

"Nothing," said David. "He does that kind of thing all the time."

Grandpa looked at what we spread out on the table. "So, young scientists, now that we know what we have, what else do you think we need?"

"Probably some cocoa and milk," said Emily. "Do you want me to go upstairs and get some?"

"No. I don't think that's a good idea," said Grandpa. "If you go upstairs for cocoa and milk, your parents might think we're done and make all of you go upstairs." Grandpa turned to Deacon Strong. "Mike, would you mind running to the store to get us more?"

Deacon Strong nodded as he pulled his car keys out of his pocket. "Cocoa and milk, anything else?"

"How about a few more Bunny's Best marshmallow rabbits," I said as I tipped my head toward Emily, "because someone keeps eating them."

Emily smiled unapologetically as she popped the last bite of her marshmallow rabbit into her mouth.

Jon opened the container of lemonade and grimaced. "I think we need a new carton of Dr. Sunshine's All-Natural Lemonade. What's left in this one's been sitting out all day. I imagine it's starting to smell like that pod of elephant seals."

"May I see that carton, please, Jon?" Grandpa asked.

Jon passed it to him.

Grandpa read the ingredients and nodded. "Wow, just lemons, sugar, and water. It really is all natural. This brand should be fine to use and much easier than making it from scratch." Grandpa must've caught a whiff of what was left in the carton because he frowned. "Jon's right. This does smell bad. The seal pod is still worse, though."

Deacon Strong took a blank piece of paper from Grandpa's old notebook and made himself a list. "Be right back" he said.

While Deacon Strong shopped, Grandpa boiled some water for the cocoa in a flask over a

Bunsen burner. Jon, Emily, and I gathered the baseball gloves, baseball, and a jar to catch more fastball wind. I was about to explain to Grandpa that fanning in baseball is when the pitcher strikes out the batter – so he'd know what we were doing – but he surprised me when he spoke first.

"You know I just made the connection. You needed something related to spring to fan the clouds back to the ocean, so you used Griffin's Greatest Fastball. Strikes them out every time. Impressive and very creative."

"You know what fanning is?" I asked.

"Of course. I used to play baseball when I was your age. Coming to your games reminds me of those days."

Grandpa looked wistfully at my baseball glove. It was the same look he got when he sat in the stands at my games. I always thought it meant he was bored. But now I understood that it was him remembering his own baseball days. It was amazing how much new stuff I was learning about Grandpa today.

"Jon, would you mind if I catch?" Grandpa asked. "I've always wanted to try to catch one of those fastballs."

"Sure." Jon handed his glove to Grandpa.

I was a little nervous about pitching to someone his age. "You ready, Grandpa?"

"I sure am!" Grandpa stood with his feet shoulder width apart and his knees slightly bent. He held the glove on his right hand in front of his torso with the mitt facing out and ready to catch. His left hand he held behind the glove for extra support. A wide smile crossed his face – like a child waiting for a present.

"Maybe we should do a few practice tosses," I said nervously. "You know, just to make sure you're ready."

"I'm ready. Don't worry, David. You're not going to break me."

"You'd better not break either of us," said Emily as she knelt on the floor between us holding the jar.

Was there a place my parents could put me where I'd never see the light of day? If there was, that's where I'd be if I hurt either one of them, let alone both. Cautiously, I threw a pitch to Grandpa. It wasn't as hard as the ones I'd thrown to Jon.

Grandpa gave me a frustrated sigh. "Come on, David. Snowball can hit a tinsel toy and make it go faster than that. Don't go easy on me. Throw me a real Griffin's Greatest."

"You know the formula won't work right without it," Jon reminded me.

I sighed and reluctantly surrendered. "Just remember, you asked for this, Grandpa."

I wound up and threw the fastball. Grandpa caught it solidly and the impact made a "thwack" in his mitt. I was impressed. He didn't stagger at all. Another thing to add to the list of new facts about him that I was compiling today.

Grandpa took off the glove. He shook his hand back and forth like he was trying to get the blood to come back into it. "I didn't realize how much that stings. Great pitch."

"Did I hurt you, Grandpa?" I asked nervously.

"I'm fine. That was fun."

"Did you get it, Em?" Jon asked.

"No. I missed. Try again."

"Jon, why don't you take over now?" I suggested.

Grandpa held tight to the glove. "Are you kidding? I'm just getting warmed up. Let's do this."

It took some time to get enough jars of Griffin's Greatest Fastball wind for Grandpa to feel comfortable we had enough. I thought we did, but he insisted we needed more. I think he was just having fun catching.

As we stacked the jars of fastball wind on one of the shelves, Grandpa said, "You're an excellent pitcher, David. Keep throwing like that and you could match that perfect game I saw in the '56 Series."

A chill ran through me. "You *saw* that game?"

"I not only saw it, I was there. Still have my ticket stub. It was amazing."

I stood there speechless. Just hearing about that game is what inspired me to be a great pitcher, but who would ever have thought Grandpa was *there*. Before I could ask Grandpa any more questions about it, Deacon Strong was back with the groceries.

"Here you go. I got a few extra marshmallows in case they start to disappear." He gave Emily a wink.

She was already opening the package to get one. "Thanks," said Emily.

Deacon Strong chuckled. "You're welcome. What did I miss?"

"Not much. Just a little game of catch," said Grandpa. "Let's get to work."

Grandpa mixed the cocoa and placed a mug of it into the weather locker before dropping in two Snowmallows. We watched through the window. The foaming and crashing happened as usual and we saw the snow begin to fall inside the locker.

"Incredible." Deacon Strong stared in amazement at the locker. No one else said anything. "Wait...am I the only one who thinks this is cool?"

"No, sir," I said. "It's cool. It's just that we've seen it a few times already."

"I guess that makes sense." Deacon Strong sounded a little disappointed.

Grandpa leaned over to him and whispered, "I've seen it lots of times and I still think it's amazing. Never gets old for me."

Deacon Strong smiled and nodded.

Grandpa looked to me. "You're up again, David. Show me exactly what you did to make the Lemonthaw."

Jon poured a mug of lemonade while Emily lined up the other components of the formula. I tucked the chili pepper seeds (which made Grandpa itch), the cat fur (which made Jon sneeze), the soap, and the car wash sponge into a sliced marshmallow rabbit. Jon took the batteries out of the bird clock and set it for six mourning dove coos while I added the mug of lemonade, the Lemonthaw rabbit, and the last item, Griffin's Greatest Fastball, to the locker. When the cloud started to spin inside the locker, Jon replaced the batteries and set off the six o'clock chime to return the locker to clear weather. Then he took the batteries out of the clock to keep it from going off again at an inconvenient time.

Grandpa nodded approvingly. He walked toward the locker. "Hmm...Not bad. Now, let's take a closer look at the locker. I want to see if there's anything left behind by the reaction that might be a problem."

He knelt on the floor in front of the locker and looked in through the glass. Then he put his hand through the open door at the bottom and wiped his fingers around the drain. When he took his hand out, his fingers were starting to swell and turn bright red. He hurried to the sink and washed his hands.

Jon, Emily, Deacon Strong, and I waited silently. Finally, Grandpa gave us his analysis.

"Overall, not too bad. I think there are a few things we might want to adjust. First, we should think about the bird sounds. I'm still not sure if David is right about the time shift being caused by turning the clock, but the real sounds usually give a more precise result. Second, there's the issue of some scorching at the bottom of the locker. That may mean we're drying things out too much. It might be why there are so many fire danger warnings right now. Lastly, the allergy impact should be reduced. You can tell from Jon's sneezing and my scratching that it's going to be a big problem if we don't handle it."

"Now that you mention it," Deacon Strong said, "there was a segment on the radio news this morning about cat hair allergies being particularly bad right now. No one seemed to know why."

Snowball popped his head out from the box and looked at Deacon Strong with a "don't blame me" glance before turning in a half circle and going back to sleep.

"How about if we cut back on the chili peppers and the sponge," I suggested. "That should make it less dry."

"But it might not be dry enough," Grandpa said.

"We could add some allergy medication in place of them," said Jon. "The allergy medication has stuff in it to dry sinuses, so that would help with drying things out and with the allergies. Wouldn't it?"

I patted Jon on the back. "Good thinking, Jon. That just leaves the problem with the clock."

"How are we going to find a real mourning dove sound?" Emily asked. "All the birds are gone for the winter, aren't they?"

"No. Not all mourning doves migrate," said Deacon Strong.

Jon nodded. "He's right. And, there's a nest in the rhododendron outside your dining room window. I noticed it when we were searching the house for spring things yesterday."

I lifted an eyebrow at him. "But you still brought the clock to the lab?"

Jon shrugged. "What was I supposed to do – open the window during a snowstorm and invite the nest of doves inside? Besides, the clock going off yesterday wasn't exactly planned."

"It was one of those God moments Deacon Strong mentioned last night," said Emily. "At least that's what I thought of when it happened."

"I don't even remember that conversation," said Deacon Strong. "Nice to know someone listened to me, though."

Emily laughed. "It's too bad you don't remember. It was kind of funny."

"Why? What else did I say?"

"You told the story about sitting on your glasses," said Emily.

Deacon Strong nodded. "Yup, Jon always thinks that one's hilarious."

"'Cause it is!" said Jon.

"Let's stay focused, everyone," Grandpa said. "It's like herding cats in here right now."

Snowball's head peeked over the side of the box again. He looked innocently at Grandpa like he was trying to say, "The cat is the one paying attention. It's the people who are all over the place."

"Sorry, Snowball. It's just an expression," said Grandpa. "Go back to sleep."

Snowball lay back down in the box as if he were satisfied with the apology. By that time, the rest of us were focused and waiting for instructions.

"We're ready, Grandpa," I said. "What do we do now?"

"First, let's try the changes to the formula for the dryness and see if they work. Then we'll figure out the bird clock after that."

Once again, we mixed a mug of cocoa, put it in the locker, and added the Snowmallows. Then Jon, Emily, and I added an adjusted Lemonthaw rabbit to the locker. But, before we were able to set off the mourning dove sounds, the hourly chime on Deacon Strong's watch sounded. It went off at seven pm with the sound of a cuckoo.

"He has a bird call watch?" I whispered to Jon. "What is it with you guys and clocks that sound like birds?"

"Until this week, they were never a problem," said Jon.

I groaned. "Point taken."

On the seventh "cuckoo", Snowball jumped out of the box so quickly that he knocked it over and began racing uncontrollably around the room. As the box shifted, it pushed the two brownies that were on the paper towel onto the floor.

"Well, this might be another one of those God moments, since this is the other part of what we need to show you from this morning," I said.

I picked up Jon's bird clock, turned it ahead to seven o'clock, and replaced the batteries. Seven eagle screeches followed the cuckoos. Snowball instantly calmed down, but the wind inside the locker started to kick up again. I took the batteries out of the bird clock and turned it back to six, but, before putting the batteries back in, I stopped.

"Grandpa, I'm afraid to do this again. What happens if all of us forget what happened after I put the batteries back in?"

"Well, our choices are to either set off the six o'clock chime or be destroyed by a tornado. Personally, I think the clock is the better option. Besides, the three of you didn't forget what happened when you did this before."

He was right. I put the batteries back into the clock and set off the six o'clock mourning doves. As the fifth Coo sounded from the clock, I crossed my fingers and waited.

CHAPTER 25

Thursday, March 7 – Early Evening

The tornado in the locker subsided at the sound of the sixth Coo.

"Is everybody good?" I asked.

"I think so," said Emily and Grandpa at the same time.

Emily smiled. "Jinx, you owe me a soda!"

Jon rubbed his forehead. "Where am I? What happened? Where have I been the past week?"

Deacon Strong looked nervously between Jon and me as I grabbed Jon's shoulders. "Jon, we're in the lab trying to fix the Snowmallows. Don't you remember?"

Jon gave his snorty laugh. "Yeah, I remember. I was just messing with you. Someone needed to lighten the mood around here."

I pushed his shoulders away. "Seriously? You thought that would *lighten* the mood? That was NOT funny."

"I have to go with David on this one," said Deacon Strong. "Please don't scare me like that."

Jon's smile melted away. "Sorry. I was just joking."

I breathed a heavy sigh as I tried to refocus. "Now, what time is it?"

Grandpa and Deacon Strong checked their watches. They were both behind by an additional hour, as were their cell phones. Grandpa gave a thoughtful nod. "Interesting. I think we can safely say that turning the clock after the cuckoo sounds is the cause of the time shift."

Snowball blinked at Grandpa with a "Ya think" look before jumping back into the spring stuff box.

"Mike, do me a favor and turn off the hourly chime on your watch," said Grandpa to Deacon Strong. "And, David, please take the batteries out of the bird clock again. We don't want either one going off while we're experimenting."

Grandpa didn't have to tell me twice. I quickly removed the batteries as Deacon Strong hit some buttons on his watch.

Grandpa picked up his pad and paper. "In the meantime, I'll jot some notes about the difference between the current time on my watch and the actual, correct time. Later, we'll need to know that information to adjust back to the right time."

Jon put his hand through the locker door and wiped his fingers around the drain at the bottom. "There still some scorching around the drain, but I'm not itchy or sneezing. Guess that's why it's called Sneezy and Itchy's allergy medication."

Grandpa looked over his glasses at Jon and then looked back down and continued writing. "That's good news. That means we're moving in the right direction with our formula components."

"What do we do now?" asked Emily.

"That's a good question," Grandpa said. "Personally, I think we need to collect the natural sound of some actual mourning doves."

"How do we do that?" asked Deacon Strong.

"Well, thanks to Jon, we know where to find some," I said. "Maybe we could bring them inside?"

Without looking up from his notes, Grandpa said, "No, the sound needs to be coming from their natural setting."

"But you never know when you'll hear them. We can't sit outside all night waiting for them to coo," said Deacon Strong.

Emily's face brightened. "Jon, didn't you say the other day that the mourning dove is one of the bird calls you know?"

"Sure, but it's still not a natural sound," said Jon.

I understood where her thought was going, so I jumped in. "But, didn't you also say they answer you back sometimes?"

Jon smiled. "Most of the time, actually."

"So that means we don't need to sit around waiting for them," I said. "We'll make them answer us."

Deacon Strong looked proudly at Jon. "You can get them to answer you? That's pretty good, son."

I didn't think Jon could smile wider, but he did when his Dad said that.

"Excellent," Grandpa said. "However, we still need to be close to the birds to collect the sounds in the jars. That means someone is going to have to sit next to them in the dining room window."

"But, how are we going to do that with Mom and Dad home?" asked Emily.

I scratched my head. "We're going to have to create a distraction. But it's going to have to be long enough to give us time to collect some jars of mourning dove coos."

"Jon, how long does it take for the mourning doves to answer when you call?" asked Grandpa.

"I don't know. A couple minutes, maybe."

Grandpa did some calculations on his pad. "We should collect at least ten jars to be safe. That means we should allow about 15 to 20 minutes to collect everything."

"Anyone have any ideas about how we can distract them that long?" I asked.

Emily's hand was in the spring stuff box petting Snowball. "I have an idea, but Snowball's not going to like it."

Emily had my attention. "What's your idea, Em?"

"I think we should get Snowball dirty."

This time she lost me. "Emily, this is no time to kid around."

"I'm not kidding. If Snowball gets dirty, Mom and Dad will have to help me clean him. That means he'll need a bath and a brushing. His fur is long, so it'll take at least 20 minutes."

"But you don't necessarily need both your Mom and your Dad to help clean Snowball, so we need something more than that," said Deacon Strong.

"How about if both of you get dirty?" I suggested.

Panic flashed in Emily's eyes. "Now, wait a minute. I don't want to get dirty."

I gave her a playful pat on the back. "Come on, Em. Take one for the team."

Jon raised his hand enthusiastically. "Dibs on the shoes!"

"No! Not my shoes! Doesn't anybody have another idea?"

"Emily," said Grandpa, "It is a good plan. It'll make sure both your parents are kept busy. While one is cleaning Snowball, the other will be cleaning your shoes."

Emily's brow furrowed. "Not my shooooes!"

"You want them to be distracted for as long as possible, don't you?" asked Jon. "Besides, those shoes have been crying for some dirt."

Jon gave Emily a sneaky smile and started creeping toward her. She tried to keep away from him. Jon shifted quickly from side to side. Emily matched his moves on the opposite side of the table until...Splat! She stepped on one of the super fudgy brownies that Snowball had knocked on the floor. The extra chocolate bits were still melty and left a squishy brown mess around her shoe.

Emily's mouth puckered. "Yuck!" she said. When she lifted her foot, most of the smashed brownie dropped from it back onto the floor with a plop, but there was still enough stuck to the shoe and the bottom tread so that it would be tough to clean.

"Told you I had the shoes," said Jon. He picked up one of Grandpa's umbrellas. "Now, come on over to the bookshelves and bring Snowball so I can help you two with the rest of your disguise."

"You're enjoying this, aren't you?" I asked.

"Are you kidding? I've been waiting a while to see that kid get dirty. This is the most fun I've had in a week. Come on, Emily; it's too late to turn back now."

Emily looked down at her messy shoe. I could tell she was resisting the urge to cry. "Darn old extra chocolate bits." She took off the dirty shoe, picked up Snowball, and carried him to the bookshelves. "Fine. Let's get this over with."

Jon shielded his nose and mouth, tipped one of the top shelves with the umbrella, and a whoosh of dust fell on top of her and Snowball. I rubbed the dust into Snowball's fur to mess him up even more. Snowball's low-pitched growl was my clue to stop.

"I think that ought to do it," I said. "Let's get to work."

I handed Emily her messy shoe. She grabbed it with a couple of free fingers as she held Snowball in her arms. With one shoe on and one shoe off, she stomped lopsidedly up the stairs.

As I watched her go, I felt kind of sorry for her because, if Snowball was going to growl and be a problem, it might take both Mom and Dad to clean him. Maybe we could have saved her shoes, but the damage was already done.

Jon, Grandpa, and Deacon Strong got some empty jars off the shelves while I listened at the bottom of the stairs for the cue from Emily.

CHAPTER 26

Thursday, March 7 – Evening

"**M**om! Dad! There's something wrong with Snowball!" Emily sounded like she was crying when she reached the top of the stairs. Was that real or part of the act? Considering how she looked a few minutes prior, the tears were probably real.

"What's wrong, baby?" asked Mom.

"Snowball started running around the lab for no reason. There must be something wrong with him."

"Don't worry," said Dad. "Cats do that sometimes, especially around certain smells. Grandpa just got back from a new place, so maybe Snowball smelled something that triggered his 'catnip senses'."

"No! There's something wrong with him. I just know it. And look how dirty he is. And how dirty I am. And worst of all, look what happened to my shoe!"

"Wow!" Dad said. "Something big must've happened for your shoe to get dirty. By the way...what is that brown stuff all over it?"

"Stupid brownies."

Mom breathed a sigh of relief. "Oh, thank goodness. I was worried there was something bigger wrong with the cat."

"There *is* something wrong! You're doctors. You have to help him," said Emily.

"Shh," said Mom. "Calm down, baby. We'll take him into the bathroom and clean him up. Then Dad can give him an exam while I clean your shoe."

"Can we use the bathroom in your room? It's bigger in case he starts running around again."

"Sure. By the way, you look awfully dirty, too. Maybe you should take a shower while we take care of Snowball," Mom said.

"No! I want to stay with him!"

"Take a deep breath, Emily," said Dad. Emily made the same stuffy sounding breath she made last night before bed. "Feel better?"

"Yes." Emily sounded calmer.

"Now, let's go have a look at him," said Dad.

"Everything's going to be fine," Mom said.

"Are you sure?" Emily's voice trailed off as they headed down the hall, through Mom and Dad's room, and into the master bathroom.

Emily was amazing. She was the most promising actor of all of us. I went back into the lab. "She did it. The coast is clear. Time to man our posts."

The plan was simple. Deacon Strong and I were going to sit in the dining room with the empty jars. We would open the window just above the doves and try not to startle them. Grandpa and Jon would be outside. Grandpa was going to stand near the street looking up at the dining room window. Jon was going to be around the corner of the house closest to the window so he could call to the doves. It was a good spot where no one could see him if they heard the noise and looked out another window. When

* 229 *

Deacon Strong and I were ready, I would signal Grandpa by turning off the dining room light. Then, since Jon couldn't see the window, Grandpa would signal Jon by turning on a flashlight. Jon would then sound the mourning dove's cry and Deacon Strong and I would catch the dove's response in the jars. It wasn't a perfect plan, but hopefully it would work.

While Deacon Strong and I were waiting for Grandpa to reach his spot near the street, I needed to ask him a question.

"Deacon Strong, there's something I've been wondering. Last night you told us the story about how you lost your glasses to show Emily that, when we pray, God doesn't always answer us in the ways we expect."

"She mentioned something about that. What's on your mind?"

"Well, I said a prayer after that asking God to help me with what I needed to fix."

"That's good. Did he answer?"

"That's the part I don't understand. I thought I got the answer when I found the stuff about the

Chinook, but then the clock went crazy and messed things up even more."

"I see."

"So, I'm wondering why God didn't help me fix things? I mean, I get that it might not happen the way I expect, but shouldn't he have done *something* to help? Or did I do something so bad that he won't even listen to me?"

Deacon Strong gave me a serious look. "Listen to me, David. There is *nothing* you can *ever* do that will make God stop listening to your prayers. He loves you too much for that. Besides, you said you thought he helped you find the information on the Chinook. Maybe there were still other things that needed fixing besides the Snowmallows."

At that moment, Grandpa came into view near the street. Seeing him made me realize that I felt closer to him than I had in a long time. "Maybe you're right. Maybe there were other things. Thanks."

"Are you ready?" asked Deacon Strong.

"Ready."

I gave Grandpa the signal. Grandpa signaled Jon and soon we could hear Jon around the corner making the distinctive cooing sound of the doves. After two or three of Jon's attempts, the doves finally began to respond. Deacon Strong and I captured the real dove cries in the jars each time they cooed back. When we'd used up all the jars, we signaled to Grandpa by turning the dining room light back on and then we headed back to the lab. About ten minutes later, Emily and Snowball joined us.

"What's the matter, Em?" I asked when I saw her long face.

"Mom can't get the brownie off my shoe. The coloring in the chocolate stained it."

I gave her a hug. "I'm sorry. You did a great job, though. We got what we needed."

Emily nodded. "Good, let's get this fixed. I'm tired of lying and sneaking around."

"I agree, Em," I said, "It's time to get things back to normal."

Even though it was getting late, Jon, Emily, Grandpa, Deacon Strong, and I started revising the Lemonthaw formula. Snowball supervised from his cozy spot inside the box. He seemed happy to be clean and fluffy again because he was purring a lot when we petted him to get more fur.

Grandpa wanted us to be super precise while we adjusted the Lemonthaw formula. We started by wiping out the bottom of the locker so we could see the impact of our changes to the formula. Then we set off the Snowmallows in the locker and added our adjusted Lemonthaw ingredients to counteract it. Each time we made a change to the formula, we had to repeat these steps to make sure there were no components from the prior test that might impact the current one.

In our first round of changes, we tried reducing the number of chili pepper seeds, but then it wasn't warm enough. In round two, we added more cat fur, but Jon's allergies were getting worse. In round three, we added more allergy medication and a little bit less sponge. With each round we were sure to use the natural sound of the doves, so we didn't mess up time again.

After about an hour, Emily was sleeping with her head on the table, Snowball was starting to nip at people for petting him so much, and Jon's nose was red from blowing it. I started to worry that the formula would never be right. Then, as we added the second to last jar of mourning dove coos to the Lemonthaw in the locker, along with a more balanced combination of chili pepper seeds, cat fur, and allergy medicine, things finally started looking good. We had a formula that didn't scorch the bottom of the locker, didn't give Grandpa or Jon hives or stuffy heads, and didn't change the clocks.

Grandpa stroked the top of Emily's sleeping head and looked over at me. "I think it's time for bed now."

I was getting tired, too, but I wanted to finish. "We can't stop now. We still need to use the new formula outside, and we didn't figure out how to fix the time shift yet."

"I agree with Dr. Wilson." Deacon Strong stood up from his stool at the black-topped table. "I don't think we're going to accomplish much more tonight."

"Besides," said Grandpa, "Your parents will be looking for you soon. I think now is a good time for us to take a break and sleep on what we've done. It'll give us time to think if we missed anything before we use the new formula outside. And it'll give us time to figure out what to do about the time shift."

I stretched my arms above my head and yawned. "Maybe you're right. I am kind of tired."

I carried Snowball and Grandpa carried Emily as everyone trudged to bed.

CHAPTER 27

Friday, March 8 – Early Morning

I slept, but I didn't feel rested. I had dreams about clocks spinning out of control and cuckoo birds popping out and pecking my head. I think the worst one was the dream where Emily was crying because Snowball was bald from us petting him too much. I was relieved to wake up the next morning with Emily's fluffy, white cat sleeping calmly on the other twin bed in my room. It was only four o'clock in the morning when I woke up and I was tired, but I couldn't sleep any more. I knew those dreams weren't going to go away until all was put right with the Snowmallows. I got up, dressed, and headed to the kitchen.

Grandpa was sitting at the table, sipping his cup of coffee. "Good morning. Looks like you slept about as well as I did."

I nodded. "I had a lot of strange dreams last night."

"Me, too. I think my favorite was where I was drowning in a sea of hot cocoa and cold lemonade. The only good part was that the two mixed together were as cozy as bath water."

I laughed as I went to the refrigerator and got myself a glass of orange juice. Then I sat next to Grandpa at the table. "Grandpa, I know I said it already, but I'm really sorry I used the Snowmallows. I never thought all of this was going to happen."

"I know that. And, I want you to know that I'm proud of you for taking responsibility for what happened and for trying your best to fix it."

"Thanks."

"And, I'm glad we've gotten to spend some time together. It's been a long time since we've done that. I've enjoyed it."

"Me, too, Grandpa."

Grandpa held up his mug and I clicked my orange juice glass against it like we were toasting the idea.

"So, what do you think we should do next?" I started drinking my juice.

Grandpa swallowed a mouthful of coffee before he answered. "I think we give ourselves a couple of snow days."

I choked. A little orange juice stung the inside of my nose. I quickly wiped my face with a napkin. "Wait...What? A couple of days? Why? I thought we'd set off the Snowmallows and then use the Lemonthaw right away."

He put his mug down. "I did, too, but after I thought about it, I changed my mind. I think we need to let the Snowmallows work for a couple of days to make sure all the prior Lemonthaw effect is gone. If we don't wait for the Snowmallows to completely saturate the air, we may dry things out even more." Grandpa took the last sip of his coffee. "After all, the last time you had a snow day, you didn't really get to enjoy it, did you?"

"Well, that's true. I guess it's settled. What are we waiting for?"

I mixed some cocoa in the kitchen while Grandpa went downstairs to get the mugs and the Snowmallows. When he came back up, he also had the baseball gloves and the ball.

"What are those for?" I asked.

Grandpa shrugged. "I thought we could play some catch before the snow really gets going. It'll give us a chance to clear our heads and figure out how to solve the time shift."

"Works for me."

We poured the cocoa into the mugs. Grandpa carried them while I brought the Snowmallows and the baseball stuff. We set everything on the porch railing.

"You used four Snowmallows the other day, right?" Grandpa asked.

"Yes."

"Well, let's do that again. The dryness still in the air should keep the storm from being as bad as last time, but we should still get enough snow to get rid of any impact from the original Lemonthaw." Grandpa took out four Snowmallows from the bag. "Would you like to do the honors?"

I put my hands up in front of me like someone trying to block a stray pitch. "No, thanks. That didn't go so well for me the last time."

Grandpa nodded. "I get it."

He dropped two Snowmallows into each mug. It took a little bit longer for the foaming to start than the last time, but soon there was a "crash" followed by light flurries.

"Now we wait," said Grandpa as he handed me a glove. "Just wish I knew for how long."

As we tossed the ball back and forth, Grandpa said, "This is a strange combination of our favorite things. Don't you think?"

I nodded. "I'm not sure I've ever played catch in the snow before."

"Me either."

As we played, I thought of something I'd wanted to ask Grandpa for a long time. Even though I was feeling more comfortable around him, I still wondered if I should ask. I thought quietly for a few moments.

"Penny for your thoughts," said Grandpa.

"Grandpa, I want to talk to you about something, but..."

"But, what?"

"But I'm not sure how you'll react."

"Well, let's do this. You ask me your question. I promise not to get upset, but, if I don't want to answer, I'll tell you. How does that sound?"

"I guess that's fair."

"So, what's on your mind?" asked Grandpa.

"Grandpa, why do you like winter so much?"

"That's an acceptable question. Before I answer, may I ask why you want to know?"

I frowned. I wondered if that option not to answer applied to both of us. But I swallowed hard and told him the truth. "Because I've always been a little mad at you that you still liked winter after what happened to Grandma."

Grandpa almost dropped the ball. "Is that why you stopped visiting the lab?"

I nodded. "I'm sorry, but I think what happened the day she died is why I don't like winter or marshmallows or science."

"Huh," said Grandpa. I could tell he was thinking about my answer and about what to say next. "David, I'm sorry that you felt that way. I always wondered what made you stay away from the lab. I figured it had something to do with Grandma, but I never knew how to ask about it. I guess that means there was something I wanted to ask you for a while, too."

I smiled. Maybe Grandpa and I were more alike than I thought.

He tossed me the ball. "Do you like winter or science or marshmallows now that you've been working in the lab with them for a few days?"

"I don't know...maybe a little." It was funny. A few days ago, I never would have said that. "So, will you tell me why you still like winter?" I asked.

"For starters, I've always preferred the cold weather. But I guess I mostly like winter because it's what brought Grandma and me together in the first place."

"That makes sense."

"You know, Grandma used to tell me that she felt cheated a little bit by being raised in Florida."

"Really?" I asked. "Why?"

"The weather there was mostly the same all year round, so people kept their regular schedules. Up here, on the other hand, a good solid snow day gave everyone a chance to stop and relax by a nice crackling fire with their families. She said that it seemed like time moved a little more slowly up here in the winter. She thought that helped people reflect on what was really important."

"I'll agree with time moving slow in winter. Sometimes I feel like winter's never going to end! Then we get into spring and summer and they fly by."

"I hear you, but I think Grandma was right. It's nice to slow things down a bit before you have to 'Spring Forward' into all the busyness of the warmer months."

As Grandpa threw the ball, an idea hit me that made me miss the catch. "That's it."

"What's it? What are you talking about?"

"Grandpa, that's the answer. Spring forward...you were right about playing catch to clear our heads. I know when we're going to use the Lemonthaw. Come on!"

CHAPTER 28

Friday, March 8 –
Morning

I explained my theory to Grandpa on the way to the lab.

"Our problem starts when the cuckoo sounds before the bird clock when we're using the Lemonthaw, right?"

"That's our theory," said Grandpa.

"So, why don't we make Lemonthaw bunnies without the mourning dove sounds in them? We can use them first. Then we set off the cuckoo clock. After that, we'll set the bird clock to the correct time and make it go off. Last, we'll release the actual mourning dove coos from the jar. That order should fix the time and stop the Snowmallows."

"Good theory, but what does that have to do with springing forward?"

"On a small scale like the lab, it should work anytime. But on the larger scale outside, we might need a little more help. Emily mentioned that we turn the clocks ahead this weekend because of Daylight Saving Time..."

Grandpa finished my sentence. "So, if we set off the reactions when everyone's clocks are set to move forward anyway, it's more likely to be successful. And two days should be enough time to let the Snowmallows work to erase all the prior Lemonthaw impact. Good thinking, David! I knew there was a scientist in you."

"Thanks, Grandpa."

"Just to be safe, we should test it in here first," said Grandpa.

Grandpa and I spent some time in the lab gathering up the needed ingredients to see if we had enough of everything. If not, Grandpa would have to go to the store before the snow got worse. Some of the things were starting to run low, but, fortunately, there was still enough of everything for one test in the lab and the actual fix outside. I kept my fingers crossed, though, because we would be in big trouble if the test didn't work the first time.

As we were getting ready to put the mugs of cocoa in the locker, the door to the lab flew open. Jon and Deacon Strong rushed in followed by Emily and Snowball. Jon's uncombed hair was sticking out in strange directions, Deacon Strong looked like he hadn't shaven, and Emily was still in her pajamas.

"Good Morning," said Grandpa. "It looks like we all had a rough night's sleep."

Snowball stretched a long stretch with his front paws down low in front of him and his tail end in the air. He hopped onto the table and rubbed on Grandpa's outstretched hand.

"I take that back," said Grandpa, "It looks like at least one of us is awake this morning."

"What happened? Why is it snowing again?" asked Emily.

"I really hope this is because of something we know about and not a new problem we have to fix," Jon said.

I shook my head at him. "You of little faith. Don't worry. Grandpa and I set off the Snowmallows."

"Why would you do that?" asked Jon. "Did you forget how much trouble they were the first time?"

"Relax, Jon. Grandpa and I think we know how to correct them and the time. We were just about to test our theory."

"What do you need us to do?" Deacon Strong asked.

"Praying might help," I said.

Jon's eyes opened wide. "Really?"

I nodded. "Faith and science aren't mutually exclusive, you know."

Jon laughed and shook his head.

I turned to Deacon Strong. "I thought about doing it myself, but I might mess it up again. I'm going to leave it to someone with more experience."

Deacon Strong chuckled. "I'm sure you'd be fine if you tried. But, if it makes you feel better, I can handle that. Actually, I've been praying since last night."

"Keep it up," I said. "I think it's helping."

Emily gathered more cat fur for the Lemonthaw as I placed the Snowmallows into the locker. As the snow started falling, Jon and I prepared the Lemonthaw rabbits without the mourning dove sounds. While we did that, Deacon Strong set his watch so he could play the cuckoo chime at any time just by pressing a button. Grandpa set the bird clock to the current incorrect lab time which was still behind by one hour from real time. I put a mug of lemonade into the snowy locker and added the Lemonthaw rabbits. As the small tornado began to form inside the locker, Deacon Strong pressed the button on his watch. It only took one cuckoo from the watch for Snowball to jump from the box and onto the floor. He circled the table making a whirlwind of his own. Grandpa replaced the batteries in the bird clock and turned it forward one hour to what the correct time should be. Seven eagle screeches sounded. Then, I released the mourning dove coos from the jar. At the sound of the final coo, all was quiet in the locker and in the lab.

"Did it work?" asked Emily.

Deacon Strong and Grandpa rubbed their foreheads like they were rubbing away a headache.

"I remember what happened this week," said Deacon Strong.

"I do, too. I really was flying upside down in a plane. That's a memory I'd like to forget."

Grandpa and Deacon Strong took their cell phones out of their pockets. Both were now set to the correct time.

"Thank Heaven," said Deacon Strong.

I sighed. "That means it worked in here. Now let's hope it will work outside."

CHAPTER 29

Sunday, March 10 – Very Early Morning

The Snowmallows Grandpa and I used outside worked well enough to cancel school on Friday. As it snowed on Friday and Saturday, Jon, Emily, Grandpa, and I fine-tuned what needed to be done at 2 a.m. on Sunday. That was the hour when Daylight Saving Time would spring everyone forward.

Since Grandpa and Deacon Strong's memories were already corrected by the fix in the lab, we decided that Jon, Emily, and I should set off the correction outside. Grandpa was concerned that the two of them would get stuck in a new time paradox if they were outside when the fix occurred. The insulation of the lab was their best protection.

There was only one jar of mourning dove coos left after our test in the lab, so we ran practice drills, without setting off any actual Snowmallows or Lemonthaw, until everyone was comfortable with the steps we needed to take outside. Before we knew it, Sunday morning arrived.

Fortunately, Mom and Dad were working again, like they did with the last storm, so there was no problem with Emily and me being in the lab with Grandpa at 1 a.m. – or rather 10:30 p.m. Snowmallow time. When Mrs. Strong fell asleep, Deacon Strong and Jon snuck downstairs to the lab.

We practiced the drill one more time. Then, Grandpa gave us some final reminders. "Now, remember, it was 8:30 when you turned the clocks to correct for the cuckoo on Thursday morning. That reset the clocks back to 6 a.m. I reconfirmed that difference between my cell phone and the upstairs clocks a few minutes ago. So, be sure you correct the time on the bird clock by two and a half hours before you open the jar of mourning dove coos."

Jon smirked. "Those have to be the weirdest instructions ever. Scares me that I understand them."

"Don't worry, Grandpa. We've got this," I said. "What time is it now?"

Deacon Strong looked at his cell phone. "Ten minutes until two." Grandpa nodded in agreement.

I shrugged. "Then I guess it's time."

Jon, Emily, and I went out to the front porch. We had Snowball's box from the lab filled with the mugs, the lemonade, the Lemonthaw rabbits, the bird clock, and the last jar of mourning dove coos. We also had Deacon Strong's watch, which was still set to the cuckoo chime. Snowball followed behind us as if he wanted his box back.

Quickly we set up what we needed according to our rehearsal in the lab. One minute before the chime on the watch was to sound 2 a.m., Jon poured Lemonade into the mugs from a sealed pitcher and Emily dropped in the Lemonthaw rabbits.

Foaming...crashing...wind...and then the watch. "Cuckoo, Cuckoo". Snowball darted back into the house as I turned the bird clock forward a half hour to set off twelve owl hoots. The wind began to pick up. Then I turned the clock forward again, this time by one hour. A single "cock-a-doodle-doo" brought us to one o'clock. The wind grew into a swirling funnel. I adjusted forward one more hour. Just as the clock finished clucking twice, Snowball came charging onto the porch leaving a trail of flying fur behind him. Jon stood by the porch railing near the stairs and was opening the jar of mourning dove coos when the fur caught his nose. Jon sneezed. He dropped the jar over the side of the porch. It hit the blue pointed hat of the garden gnome and shattered. A jumble of mourning dove coos rose from the shards all at once.

I panicked. "Oh, no! Now what do we do?"

The swirl of the tornado continued to intensify until suddenly... "Coo, coo, coo-hoo-oo". The mourning doves next to the dining room window responded to the sounds that jumbled out of the jar. Soon doves from trees and soffits all around the neighborhood joined the chorus. Instantly, the tornado vanished. Snowball calmed down, jumped back into his box, and curled up to sleep. Best of all, the snow was gone, and the sky was clear.

I shook my head in amazement. "I'd call that a God moment."

Jon and I hurried to the lab to check on Grandpa and Deacon Strong. Emily followed behind us carrying Snowball in the box. The insulation in the lab did its job. They were fine.

"How can we be sure it worked?" I asked.

Grandpa's cell phone rang. "Hello?"

"Dad?" It was my Mom's voice. "I know two in the morning – well, three with the Daylight Saving Time change – is an odd time to call, but I had a strange feeling I should check on things."

"Everything's fine. Why were you concerned?"

"Well, it looks like this freak snowstorm just did the same thing as the one we had earlier in the week. I was a little worried that something went wrong in your lab."

Grandpa gave me a wink. "Audra, I can assure you that, right now, everything in my lab is fine."

"And the kids?"

"Safe and sound."

"That's good. I keep feeling like I'm supposed to be upset with them for some reason. I must've dreamt that I grounded them. Silly, huh?"

"You've been working a lot of hours with all these storms. That can take a toll on anyone."

"That's true. Sorry if I woke you. I'll be home after the workers for the morning shift arrive."

"No problem. Thanks for checking in. Love you."

"I love you, too, Dad."

Grandpa hung up the phone. "I think we have our answer."

I nodded and smiled.

Emily and Jon exchanged a high five, a low five, and a jog in place for a count of five as Deacon Strong looked on. Snowball slept peacefully in his box.

Grandpa turned to me. "It looks like you'll get to take that science test after all. And, after this last week, I think you'll pass. Looks like baseball season's been saved."

"Thanks to you," I said.

"You figured out most of it on your own. I'm proud of you." Grandpa lifted his hand to shake mine, but I went one better. I taught Grandpa the victory handshake and followed it with a hug.

"I guess you'd better get out on that baseball field and get in some practice," said Grandpa when I finally released him from the hug.

"I will after I study a little more. There's still a couple of things I don't quite understand. Will you help me?"

"With studying? Sure," said Grandpa.

"No, with both," I said. "And maybe while we're at it, you could tell me more about that game in '56?"

Grandpa tipped his head down slightly and looked at me over the top of his glasses. "I'd love that."

"Me, too, Grandpa."

CHAPTER 30

Saturday, March 16 – Afternoon

"It's a beautiful day here at Fairlane Park for game seven of the Snowmallow Series." Jon stood at the pitcher's mound. He held a pretend microphone to his mouth. "It's the bottom of the ninth. Score is tied. Two outs, with a man on base."

"So, you're the announcer now?" I asked. "What the matter? Afraid to play? Afraid you're going to lose to me and my grandfather?"

"Nope. Your grandfather has you as a handicap, so I think Dad, Emily, and I are pretty safe," answered Jon.

"I'm not a handicap. I got an A on my weather test, didn't I?"

"Yeah, but you only got a C plus in science for the marking period."

"I passed," I said. "That's all that matters. And I'm going to do better next time. Grandpa's going to help me."

"Are you boys going to stand there and talk all day? Or are we going to play some ball?" Emily shouted at us from the outfield. She was wearing a new pair of clean white sneakers. Her long ponytail stuck out of the hole in the back of her pink baseball cap. Snowball was chasing butterflies nearby.

"She's right. Let's get on with the game," said Deacon Strong. He was covering third. I was standing safely on the base next to him. "Emily's in a hurry to get her shoes dirty."

"No, thank you," she answered.

Grandpa stepped to home plate. "Guess I'm up."

I cheered him on. "Come on, Grandpa. One more run and we win. Remember what I told you."

Jon looked over at me and raised a suspicious eyebrow. "Everybody be ready. Sounds like

Dave's been coaching him, so he's probably going to hit to the outfield."

Deacon Strong and Emily spread out further. Grandpa took his stance. Jon wound up and tossed the pitch...and Grandpa bunted. I crossed home plate easily for the winning run.

I ran over to Grandpa and exchanged a high five, a low five, a jog in place for five, and a hug.

After the game, Jon shook his head in disgust. "You bunted, Dr. Wilson?"

"Of course. I've been waiting to use that play since David first told me about it. Now, come on. Let's celebrate with some sodas – my treat. Besides, I still owe one to Emily."

"Hurrah! Does that mean I get two?" Emily asked as she, Grandpa, and Deacon Strong started walking toward home. Snowball ran to catch up with Emily. Jon and I quickly gathered the bats and balls but were still several steps behind the rest of the group.

"I can't believe I fell for that again," said Jon.

"Don't feel bad, Jon. You know I'm..."

"Full of surprises. Yeah, I know," said Jon.

I laughed. "Yup." Then, I looked at the group walking in front of us. "And, you know, the biggest surprise of all?"

Jon shook his head.

"The biggest surprise," I said, "is that Grandpa and I make such a great team."

Acknowledgements

Thank you. Thank you to all of you who had any part in helping with the production of this book. Snowmallows has been in progress since the late 1990's and has transformed from a 4,000 word writing assignment to the over 40,000 word manuscript it is today. So, as you can imagine, there have been many people who have helped and supported this effort over the years – fellow writers, fellow readers, instructors of courses and webinars, people who have given me helpful critiques, and family, friends, and neighbors who have shared their gifts and skills with me. I thank every one of you for your time and expertise. I would love to mention each person individually, but in the interest of not adding another 200 pages to this book, I will mention only a few of you specifically. However, please know that if you helped in any small way through encouragement, prayer, or other assistance – I thank you sincerely.

So, let's begin at the top. Thank you, God, for your Word, for the Word made Flesh, and for the words you've allowed me to write. I offer this work to you and I hope you are pleased with it.

Thanks to my wonderful husband, Don, for being my biggest supporter in all my endeavors. You helped make this dream a reality.

Thank you to my Mom, Dad, and brothers who gave me a wonderful childhood in which to dream, but also a good work ethic and the sense to keep my feet on the ground. I believe all these qualities are crucial to self-publishing. Thanks to the rest of my family, too. You have provided unlimited encouragement through the years.

I've also had the wonderful intercession of many saints in heaven – both named and unnamed. (I know you're up there, Mom, because, since last year, there have been many God moments in the process of publishing this book.) I could not have done it without them.

Thanks to some friends who made an extra special difference in the creation of this book: to

Sharon for inspiring the idea through "the power of the cocoa"; to Cay for helping me decide that Grandpa needed to become a real character in the story and not just a sub-plot; to Melinda for taking the "about the author" photo; and to Patti and to Kate for generously sharing their editing gifts. I greatly appreciate your time and talent.

I would like to acknowledge the use of the templates for the interior of the book from BookDesignTemplates.com and the cover design by Katrina through Design Crowd. These services made bringing the book to life much easier. Various services of Amazon, Ingram Spark, Adobe, Design Crowd, and the program calibre may also have been used in the production of certain copies of this book.

Finally, I thank you – the reader – for the gift of your time. As Grandpa pointed out, time is a fragile and important gift. I am honored and humbled that you chose to spend some of yours with me. God bless you!

ABOUT THE AUTHOR

Carol Ann Soisson writes from her home in
Connecticut – where they know a little bit about
snow. She's published spiritual meditations for
adults. This is her first book for children.

Made in the USA
Middletown, DE
24 July 2021

44395589R00163